5/28/11

Dear sister in the Le[illegible]
you are such a fun [illegible]
to know + love. I'm glad
paths crossed on this earth.

Joanne

FISHING WITH *Cinnamon Rolls*

"A Widow Does Strange Things"

DR. JOANNE NELSON KING BROWN

authorHOUSE®

AuthorHouse™
1663 Liberty Drive
Bloomington, IN 47403
www.authorhouse.com
Phone: 1-800-839-8640

First published by AuthorHouse 2/22/2011

ISBN: 978-1-4567-4834-0 (e)
ISBN: 978-1-4567-4835-7 (dj)
ISBN: 978-1-4567-4836-4 (sc)

Library of Congress Control Number: 2011902988

Printed in the United States of America

Cover illustration by George Massey.

This book is printed on acid-free paper.

Dedicated to my three sons, Timothy, Thomas, and Michael, who ate my leftover cinnamon rolls, and to the kind, handsome trucker man who "took the bait" and stayed to eat cinnamon rolls for the rest of his life. He made my life worth living.

I love you fellas.

Gratefully,
A Widow Lady

PREFACE

Luke 8:39 is the reason for this book: "Return to your own house and tell what great things God has done for you."

Also Psalm 102:18: "Write this down for the next generation, so people not yet born will praise God."

With a sense of awe, I have written what I hear the Spirit telling me. I find that God has a very good sense of humor. This is a retelling of real life as experienced by a young widow left with three young boys. A few names have been changed due to the fact that some people are still living this side of heaven and did some mighty dumb things. I do not wish to embarrass them.

I prayed daily, "Make my actions worthy of imitation." But I still failed often. The reader needs to keep in mind that this book took place over an eight-year period. At first, I had three children home, then two, then one, and at the last, I was left alone. During this period, God was as real to me as He has ever been in my life. God's promise to John that He would help me raise the boys in his absence was seen in the reality of our daily lives and the boys' adult lives now. Also, it was seen in crisis after crisis as they were growing up.

Psalm 91:11 reads, "For He orders His angels to protect you wherever you go." You will see His protection in many scary situations in this book.

Also, Psalm 18:32 assured me and was oh, so true many a dangerous time. "He fills me with strength and protects me wherever I go."

CONTENTS

Chapter 1
AFTER THE FUNERAL

Being alone can be a scary thing!

As I crawled into the big, king-size bed and sprawled out from one side to the other, I began to learn the feeling of sleeping single in a double bed. I was a queen sleeping in a king-size bed without my king. However, the roominess was pleasing.

Not bad, actually, I thought.

When the last visitor of the day left and the boys were in their rooms preparing to retire, I happily went to my room to be alone with God and receive comfort and companionship from the Holy Spirit. People thought I ought not be by myself the first night after John died, but I was anxious to be alone with God and feel His presence near. My mind was numb for a while, and I just seemed to exist. Then I began to feel safe and protected, almost more than when I had an earthly mate to protect me. It was a wonderful feeling! Now that it was just God, the three boys, and me to face the world, I had some serious thinking to do. First on my list was to figure out "Who am I?"

I was no longer the preacher's wife, nor was I "John King's wife," nor was I a wife at all. I was not a missionary, just a former missionary. I now had to lay aside my former life and reconstruct my life once again. What did God want me to do with this life I had left? How was I going to work out, "Jesus living in me, the hope of glory"?

God made me a woman, living on planet Earth. I had the hormones, the desires, the passions, and the eyes of a woman. I knew that daily I must filter all of the above through God's love for me and my desire to please Him. I knew that when I failed, His gracious hand was held out to me to restore me to His fellowship. I was aware that His blood washed over me and made me pure so I could be His ambassador to all around me.

How was I going to be able to raise my boys for the Lord so they could be aware of God's Spirit inside them and let Him do His work in their lives? I was well aware of the old saying, "You can't purify the water by painting the pump." I needed to get inside their hearts and heads and then leave the rest to the Lord.

Before I went to sleep that night, I had figured out that I was, like it or not, the earthly head of this household. It would be my personal responsibility to make sure a roof was over our heads, food on the table, and clothes on our backs. I had to take very seriously the spiritual welfare of my children. I knew I would have to dig deep within myself for what life had just thrown my way. I drifted off to sleep thinking that I had solved my problems. *How wrong I was!*

The first blow fell when I got a letter from our ministerial life insurance company. It said, "You will be getting $5.62 a month, as your policy states that John would have to die after his sixty-fifth birthday in order for the full benefits to kick in."

He was only forty-two when he died. John had thought that the boys and I would be so well taken care of, as his policy stated that we would be getting two-thirds of his salary. He was getting $850 a month when he died. Five dollars and sixty-two cents was a far cry from that.

As I sat pondering about finances, the doorbell rang.

"Hi, Joanne. I came over to talk a bit. May I come in?" Dr. Barton Dowdy smiled. He was the president of Northwest Christian College, where John and I had gone to school and where we had met and courted.

"Oh, please do!" I responded.

After I showed him the letter, he informed me, "I will spread the word and make sure the other preachers check their policies and take appropriate action if necessary." He did, and many of our pastor friends had to get new policies.

So many of our pastor friends had warned me, "Don't

make any major decisions for one year, as you are really not thinking straight."

Well, he warned me also. I, of course, thought otherwise. Why would anyone think that I was not *with it completely?* The year ahead would prove me wrong.

The first step in being financially responsible for my family was to notify everyone that John was dead. So off I trotted to the Social Security office with his death certificate in hand. Now, any of you who have been to a Social Security office know that they are not noted for their speed. I looked around the room in amazement at the variety of humanity there. I felt very out of place.

"Thank you, Dad, for coming with me. I couldn't have done this alone," I whispered in the ear of my sweet daddy.

He didn't look very comfortable either.

"A lot of people must not have access to water," I whispered.

"The body odor is making me nauseous. I could never work in here."

Two long hours later, my name was called, and off we went to sit in front of a young lady who looked much too young to know anything about the trials I was going through. She began asking questions in a very businesslike manner. Every now and then, she would put papers in front of me to sign. Tears began to flow and wet the pages she kept handing me.

How can life keep going on when my life has just fallen

apart? I asked my Heavenly Father. Then, interrupting my thoughts, I heard the young lady's voice say, "Now, you will not be working, will you?"

What did she mean, *I would not be working?*

"You cannot get paid if you continue to work. Of course, you are probably making more than what they would pay you anyway. They will pay some for the boys," she grinned.

I was ready to agree to anything just to get out of there. By now, I was close to a basket case.

When I sank into the car seat sobbing, I was so glad Dad had come along and would be driving home. That is one place you should not go alone after a death.

"Please stop by the bank, Dad, as the church gave me John's last check and I need to cash it for groceries."

I decided it would be better to go inside and try to cash it. I signed it like I always had while John was alive and handed it to the clerk. She looked at the signature and asked for ID.

"Did you sign this?" she asked.

"Yes, I always do," I honestly replied.

"Well, you will have to have him sign it himself," she said firmly, and she motioned for the next in line to come up. I did not move. This was more than I could take. I needed that money because the bank had put a stop on our checking account as soon as they found out John had died. I couldn't write a check, and now they wouldn't let me cash one either.

"My husband is dead. How do you expect me to get him

to sign it? There are no round-trip elevators to heaven," I sobbed.

All she said was, "You'll have to have him sign it."

Yeah, right, I thought.

Lord, what am I to do? I'm pleading for some help here! I informed the Lord.

As I walked back to the car, He gave me an idea.

"Dad, let's pull through the drive-through."

I slipped the check in the tube, and without any problem, the money came scooting back out. I began to cry again. Life was getting too hard for me. But it would get a lot worse before it got better.

As a rule, the mailman was my friend. Letters kept pouring in from our friends all over the world and all over the United States. I never imagined that John's and my lives had intermingled with so many wonderful, caring friends in just twenty-two short years. Their cards and letters brought me such joy.

But one day, the mailman was not my friend. He brought a note from a bank that I had never used. It said I owed them for a loan that John had taken out the day before he died. It was on a car. I had not signed any note, and John always took out that insurance that if he died it would be paid for, so I wasn't worried. *I should have been!*

I called the bank to straighten everything out. They began telling me I had a *moral* obligation to pay them. It would dishonor John's name if I didn't. So I agreed. Our budget was really going to be stretched now. Tom would need a car the next year, so this would take care of that dilemma. Tim already had a car, plus we still had John's motorcycle. I decided to put the motorcycle up for sale. That would help some. I thought that would not be a problem.

Wrong!

My neighbor wanted to buy it. I ran and got the title, only to discover the title read "John *and* Joanne King" instead of "John *or* Joanne King." I would have to either sign John's name with my left hand or have one of the boys sign his name. Left hand it was. I was thrilled to get more grocery money.

I had growing boys, and athletic ones at that. They needed their proper nourishment. We had milk delivered to the door. Three gallons twice a week, and they could have drunk more. I would buy powdered milk and mix it up when they weren't home and then add it to the regular milk. I used powdered milk to cook with almost exclusively. I bought cold cereal by the huge bag, and no one ever complained. The youngest boy could eat a mixing bowl full of cold cereal for breakfast. The middle boy ate a mixing bowl full of mashed potatoes at one sitting. The oldest boy loved tapioca and custard. These would disappear in one sitting also. All three boys were in cross country and track, so they didn't keep an ounce of fat on them.

I knew the first track meet after John died would be hard. I left work early to be sure to be there. Tim seemed to be doing fine until he was clear across the track from me, and then I saw him step off the track and go down into the grass in a heap. My heart ached for him. When he did come in, I could tell he had been crying.

"Let's go home, Mom. Dad was always at all my meets."

"I know, son."

There was no way I could be Mom and Dad too. The earthly male figure was missing in our family. He knew I was hurting too. We would all have to draw strength from one another.

I was mad at God, not only for causing me such pain but also for causing so much pain for my boys. I shook my fist in his face and told him, "How dare You!"

What a blessing it is that God is big enough to handle our little temper tantrums. He just loves us anyway. I got to demonstrate that the very next Sunday to my middle boy, Tom. We were having an argument over something. I don't even remember what it was about, but it got heated, and he left for church mad. As he sang in the choir, it was hard for him not to look down at me. I put all the love I had into a smile and winked at him. He smiled and shook his head. When we got home, he hugged me and said, "Mom, how could you smile like that at me after we had such an argument before church?"

That was God helping me to raise my boys, as he promised. Because we were struggling without our male figure, the boys and I bonded very strongly. This incident just made the glue that bonded all the stronger.

It was like the cups on a shelf at my friend's house. Two

were perfectly new, not a chip on them, and one had been glued many times. As they were having breakfast one day, the shelf fell down. They ran over to see the damage. The two new cups had broken into several pieces, but the old, glued one was undamaged.

The weekends were the worst for me. One Saturday as I came in from getting groceries, I heard Mickey call to me.

"Mom, you better come in here." *This sounds serious,* I thought. I hurriedly put the groceries down and went into the living room. There sat Michael on the sofa with a gash on his thigh about four inches long and deep enough that I could put my fist down in it. It wasn't bleeding much, and I couldn't believe it. I was freaked out, though. He didn't seem to be in a lot of pain. I feared that if I made him walk to the car, it would start to bleed.

"Mom, I walked all the way home," he reminded me. So off we headed for the hospital and the ER.

The doctor put in twenty stitches and sent us home. Tim and Tom thought it was a pretty cool wound, although Tim said, "How do you not notice a six-inch railroad spike sticking out of a car tire before you try to jump over it?" Another crisis lived through, but more were to come.

Chapter 2
THE IMPORTANCE OF ENDORPHINS

Now, I know endorphins keep you happy and healthy. I had read that a lot of widows get a serious, life-threatening disease within two years after their mates die. I didn't want to be in those statistics, so I sharpened up my sense of humor and allowed myself to laugh at myself, a lot. The Bible says, "A happy heart is good medicine." Then I discovered Philippians 1:19 *demanded* that I be glad or happy. After reading Proverbs 16:24, "Pleasant (or kind) words are like honeycomb, enjoyable and healthful," I knew I must try to make life enjoyable for my boys also. In spite of this, I did have the TV cable turned off in January to save some money. No one said anything about it. I thought they were all just being so nice. Then, that June, one of the boys told me, "Mom, the TV is broken; better get someone to fix it!"

I just sat down and began to laugh. None of them had even

missed it or known it wasn't working for six whole months. Needless to say, I didn't bother to turn it back on until fall. By then, I had changed jobs enough so that my salary was sufficient to be able to afford it.

"Paint always freshens up things, so I think it's time we give ourselves a lift, fellas. Let's go pick out some colors, and you can paint your rooms. It will be fun."

They all agreed, and we were off. Now, let me say, when a mother allows her children to pick their own room colors, she should be prepared for black, red, or purple, if need be. Or don't allow them an open-ended choice. I gambled and did allow an open-ended choice and won. All three boys picked "normal" colors that I could live with too. They, however, felt that I hadn't picked a color they wanted to live with.

"You fellas seldom come in my room anyway, and I love pink."

"Well," they informed me, "pink will assure that we won't be coming in very often."

I had read that pink was a calming color. That would be nice.

As it was just me and I didn't have to compromise with a male figure, I went for it. Of course, that meant I would need a matching bedspread and curtains, etc., etc. What fun! As I had shared a bedroom with my sister while growing up, and then a husband, this would be the first time I could design my own room. I was loving it.

The end results were great. I found it uplifting and a joy to go into. It made me smile every time I walked through the door. It was worth it.

Now, the boys did a beautiful job of painting their rooms, so I asked Tom to please paint their bathroom too. That was a shocker. When I came home from work one day and walked into their bathroom, I could not believe my eyes.

"Tom, please come here!" I yelled loud enough that he could hear me from his room with his music on.

A very defiant young man walked down the hall and said, "Yes?"

"Son, your room is just beautiful; what happened here?"

"I didn't want to paint the bathroom, so I didn't do a good job."

"That's for sure," I agreed.

At least he was honest about it. However, that bathroom doubled as our guest bathroom when we had company. It took me weeks of working on removing paint and adding paint until I felt comfortable having my friends use it.

I sat down to talk to the Lord about this situation. "How, Lord, can I help him do his best at *all* times, not just when he feels like it? That is a life lesson he must learn."

Oh, this raising boys for the Lord was so hard. I would gather my boys together in the living room, and I would read selected scriptures to them. During Tim's senior year in high school, he memorized a lot of scripture. That was very helpful to him, but I'm sure it spilled over in his attitude toward me and my struggles in trying to raise him and his brothers. I wanted to implant right and wrong in their subconscious, so they wouldn't even have to think about it but their subconscious would make the decision for them. I knew that I was not always perfect, so they must look further than me for their example. The book *What Would Jesus Do?* was out about this time, and I made sure the boys had an opportunity to read it. When they would ask me about a problem they were having, I would often answer, "What do you think Jesus would do, son?" This could be helpful in their decision-making for the rest of their lives. It was how I tried to live.

Chapter 3
FIRST CALLER FOR CINNAMON ROLLS

At work, I knew I needed to get a better-paying job. I had worked with the company day sheets, and it was fun to work with the numbers, making all the columns up and down all match. I would get so excited when they all came out right. The accountant for the Optical Shoppe said that I would be good in accounting and they would have a place for me, but he felt I would not be happy, as I seemed to be a people person and loved interacting with people. In accounting, I would be in a room all day all by myself.

After thinking it over, I was afraid he was right, so I gave up on that idea.

I needed to think about my career now and what I wanted to do to earn money for the family. I felt I needed to raise my boys before going back into a missionary position. Later

I would consider directing a Salvation Army orphanage in Guatemala, but for now, I felt I ought to stay where I was.

I heard about classes that were being given in Portland, just two hours away. I could get my National Optician's Certificate in just one year. That sounded good, but it meant leaving my boys in the evening. They assured me all would be well, so off I went out into the unknown. A lady friend from another optical office in town came with me. Sometimes a couple of the men from our Optical Shoppe went also. We would go out for pizza afterwards. Thus came about my first date after John died. It was, however, an unfortunate encounter with the male species because it came too soon after John died for any real relationship to develop.

"I'll get it!" "No, I'll get it!" rang through the house one evening as we all scrambled for the phone. It was a friend from college days who had heard of John's death and wanted me to know she had told a pastor friend in Idaho about me.

"He might be calling," she told me excitedly.

Well, I thought, *the first preacher man from Idaho certainly worked out okay. Maybe I ought to at least meet this one.*

No sooner had she hung up than the phone rang again. This time, I was close enough to get it without a lot of fuss.

"Hi, I'm Alan, and our mutual friend told me about you. I'd like to come see you."

Once a week, I was taking a night class in Portland, Oregon, at the university, and we always went out for pizza afterwards. That would be a safe place to meet him. I was not entirely comfortable with this, but heard myself telling him, "I will be at the Oregon Grinder pizza parlor in Portland on Tuesday night at nine o'clock if you want to meet me then. That would actually be closer for you than coming all the way to Springfield."

He agreed, so I described what I looked like and what I would be wearing so he could spot me easily.

My stomach began to churn and didn't stop until Tuesday night at nine o'clock. I was scared and excited and had a hard time in class but somehow made it through. We had ordered pizza and were waiting for it to get ready when a handsome man came over to our table and gently placed his hand on my shoulder. I recoiled as if a snake had bitten me. Was I ever embarrassed! The poor man introduced himself and asked if he could sit down. I had saved a place beside me, and he surely felt that spot was for him, but after my reaction to his gentle touch, he probably felt like he should turn around and go all the way back to Idaho. Poor thing, he didn't stand a chance.

He did sit down, and we began to try to talk. We soon discovered that a noisy pizza parlor was not the best place to try to get acquainted. I could hardly hear him, so he would lean over toward me to talk, and I would back away as if he had bad breath, which he didn't. My mind knew I was no longer married, but somehow, my body had not gotten the message.

"Please excuse me," I stammered. "I have worked especially hard today, then drove a hundred and fifty miles to class and took a test, which was awful, so am not really with it tonight."

Through his insistence, I accepted a date to go out to dinner with him the very next week on his day off. All my companions were really pulling for him, but it was just too scary for me. I had not even had my fortieth birthday and had no desire to get out into the dating scene yet. I'm afraid he was doomed from the start.

When our date night came the next week, he arrived at my door, and I was ready. I didn't even invite him in. How rude of me! As we rode to the restaurant, I was nearly pushing out the door on the passenger side of the car. I didn't want him to accidently touch me again, as I knew I would react badly and that would embarrass us both.

I was determined to have a good time, so was surprised to find myself so cold and stiff. In spite of that, dinner was very pleasant as I listened to his life. His wife had died over a year ago, and he missed her, of course, but wanted to get on with his life. He backpacked and loved to climb mountains. My boys would surely like that. When he brought me back home, I knew what I must do. If I didn't, it would not be fair to him.

"I'm so sorry we didn't meet a year from now, but I know I am not ready yet to even think about dating. You have many women clamoring for your attention. I wish you well, but must bow out of the competition for now. If you are still single a year from now, please do give me a call."

With that, I ran into the house and gave him the package of fresh homemade cinnamon rolls that I had wrapped up for him to eat on his trip back to Idaho. There would be many packages of cinnamon rolls put into the hands of many fine gentleman callers before the man of my dreams would come calling and stay to eat cinnamon rolls for the rest of his life.

He continued to call for a while, but the calls got further and further apart. That Christmas, I received a card from him with his and his new bride's names on it. He was a nice man. I'm sure he is happy.

Then Jim came on the scene. One date was all he could take. Clyde followed Jim and lasted as long. I felt doomed to solitude. *There will be nothing but lonely nights ahead for me,* I thought.

It sure would be nice to have a man in this household, I thought as a pedophile drove by for the third time, driving very slowly and looking at our house. I knew him from church. He had showed up at church and wanted to work with our youth, and John would not let him. The police had warned John about him. He knew I was alone with my three boys, or so he thought. Really, I had God's protection over me and my boys, but still, it was scary for me. I warned the boys, and they would look out for each other. He never got out of the car and finally drove off. Over the next few weeks, he came back a few times, but nothing ever happened. I was so grateful. Unfortunately, it did happen to one of the youth in our church. It is so hard to protect your children from those who allow the devil to rule. As I was reading my devotions one morning, 1 Peter 1:8b popped out at me.

"Even now you are happy with the inexpressible *joy* that comes from heaven itself." This he said after talking about our trials here on earth.

I wondered, *Will I ever get my joy back, the real, indescribable joy that starts at my toes and goes to the top of my head?* Then I began to reason that my joy was actually the presence of the Holy Spirit; therefore, it had nothing to do with my trials or anything outside my body. It was clear to me that 2 Corinthians 1:4 applied to me.

"God comforts us in our tribulations that we may be able to comfort those who are in trouble."

God does not comfort us to make us comfortable, but to make us comforters, I reasoned with myself.

My sister had a son in Stanford Children's Hospital, dying of cancer. She was by his side day and night. Perhaps I could go relieve her and allow her to get out for a while. So, as much as I hated to fly, I bought my ticket to San Jose, California. This would be the first time I had flown alone. Whose hand would I hold? Who would give me words of encouragement? As I walked on the plane, there sat a nice lady in the seat next to me, as if she was just waiting for me. You guessed it; she was my angel for the trip.

Now, walking the trails in the jungle of South America was not near as scary for me as walking the paved jungle streets of the big cities. But I knew I was right where God wanted me to be, and so my fear was lessened. I finally figured out that the times I became scared of life were when I was resisting doing what God clearly was asking me to do.

After I landed and rescued my luggage, I puzzled as to how to get to the hospital in Palo Alto. While I stood outside, I noticed that coming my way was a vehicle that looked like a stretch SUV and limo combined; it was actually the airport limo. When it stopped in front of me, I timidly asked the driver if he knew how I could get to Stanford Children's Hospital.

"That's not one of my stops."

My heart sank.

"But it isn't very far from where I go. Come on in and I'll take you." Relieved, I slid in next to two very nice-suited businessmen. It was a long ride, but the conversation was stimulating, and the time went fast.

"When you are ready to go back to the plane, just call me. I'll come get you." The driver smiled at me while pressing his card into my hand. That was such a wonderful relief. I could hardly believe that God had sent a limo for me. Wow!

I was not prepared for what I saw at the hospital. Little Ricky had a metal halo cast that was screwed into his head. I wondered how he could sleep. He had had surgery, and all five vertebrae were involved. As he was adopted when my sister was in Japan, the casual observer would not know that he belonged to her. In fact, the others in the room felt sorry for him, as they felt his mommy never came to see him.

"Oh, no, my mommy is here all the time," he would tell them, puzzled. He couldn't understand why they would say that. In fact, my folks, Ricky's grandma and grandpa, came down and visited too. His daddy was a chaplain in the air force and visited whenever he could, as well. My sister and I were able to walk across to the mall and relax as we window-shopped and talked. Too soon, it was time to head home. I called, and my limo came and drove me to the airport. The flight home was uneventful, and that was just fine with me. It was so good to get back home to my boys. Everything had gone well while I was gone.

One Sunday at church, a young man spoke about going to Africa on a mission. It seemed the Lord was asking me to give him the two thousand dollars that I had managed to save toward our house taxes. Now, this was a scary thought for me.

"Lord, I trust you, but are you sure this is what you want me to do? Am I understanding you correctly?"

Being the head of the household with all the bills and responsibilities was hard and very scary, and now it seemed God was asking me to give up the little cushion I had managed to stash away. How could this be?

"Trust me, Joanne," He seemed to be saying.

So I took out my checkbook and wrote a check for two

thousand dollars and presented it to the young man. I felt very good, like I had obeyed as I should.

The next day, I got home from work and was looking over the mail. There was a letter from a San Diego pharmacy. I wondered how they could have found me. We had been to South America and Texas and now were in Oregon. But there it was. I opened it with curiosity, and out fell a check. Yes, a check for two thousand dollars. It seemed, the letter read, that this pharmacy had overcharged for some medicine in 1959-1962 and now had to pay it back. Once again, the Lord let me know who was really in charge.

"I can take care of you and your boys," He seemed to be saying to me.

My boys thought they would help the Lord take care of me, especially in the man department. A friend introduced me to the superintendent of the rural schools, and he came over for tea one afternoon and to get better acquainted. My boys were home, as it was a Saturday. I was in the kitchen brewing some tea and heard conversation in the front room. When I came out with his tea, there sat one boy on his right and one on his left on the davenport. The third boy sat opposite him. I had nowhere to sit but across the room. What an awkward situation. Needless to say, he finished his tea and cinnamon rolls and left.

After he left, I quizzed my boys, "Boys, what were you trying to do?"

"Mom, we don't want a *step*dad to raise us. Please wait till we all leave home before you get remarried."

"Let's see now, that would be eight years. I'd still be in my forties and still fairly marketable." I laughed. "I'll keep that in mind."

Chapter 4

GOING IT WITHOUT A PARTNER IS SO HARD

My birthday (the fortieth one) was coming up. John always did a good job of planning a celebration, but now I had better start learning to live without much ado. To my surprise, one of the church members asked the boys and me out to dinner that night. The Johnson family was such fun to be with that I was really looking forward to the evening. They just lived right down the street from us, and the mother had gone to the hospital with me when John had his heart attack. We had just finished eating a wonderful steak dinner, and the boys had been so good. My, I was proud of them. Then … the middle boy (Tom) said, "Can we go to Farrell's Ice Cream Parlor for an ice cream sundae?"

I wanted to sink under the seat. I could simply not believe my ears as the other two boys chimed in, wanting to go get an ice cream sundae also. The friends from church agreed, of course, and we left the one restaurant and headed to Farrell's Ice Cream Parlor in the next town over. All the boys wanted to ride with the Johnsons because they were afraid of what I was going to say when I got them in the car. And I certainly would have let them know how rude that was to ask to go somewhere for an ice cream sundae. I was humiliated by the rudeness of my boys. Had I not taught them better?

I arrived at Farrell's Ice Cream Parlor and noticed several cars that I recognized from church but was too upset with my boys to even think about anything else. We all were standing in line waiting to be seated when our hosts said, "Let's just go on back to the party room."

As we approached "the party room," I began to hear familiar voices. As we entered the room, everyone sang "Happy Birthday" to me. It finally dawned on me what was happening. The church had come out to celebrate my birthday in the absence of my husband. They said they had heard John talking about giving me a surprise fortieth party, so they did it for him.

The hostess sidled up to me and whispered in my ear, "Now, don't be mad at your boys. We asked them to beg to go out to Farrell's for ice cream. We didn't know how else to get you here."

Well, that was certainly a relief!

On the way home, the boys kept telling me over and over how they had been asked to do it. My boys were such a blessing from the Lord.

What a fun party we had. They presented me with a very big, beautifully wrapped gift. I couldn't imagine what it was. As I tore open the wrapper, a handmade quilt emerged. I tried hard not to cry. I knew if the tears started, I would not be able to stop them.

Tears were to be my downfall. They are very scary when you cannot stop them. Sometimes, I felt like I was going insane and had to really try hard to hang on to my sanity. Tim would come to my rescue at just the right time and bring his date home, march right into the bedroom where I was sobbing, and say very firmly, "Mom, get your street clothes on. We're taking you out for a Coke or whatever."

I knew he was right. I needed to get out in public, and that might force me to stop sobbing. I washed my face and joined him and his date for a late-night snack. That must have been a sight! A beautiful, handsome couple gaily going into Farrell's Ice Cream Parlor, dragging behind them a teary-eyed lady whose face and eyes showed signs of a long crying binge, which no amount of splashed cold water could erase.

How grateful I was that he did that for me, because it did cause me to actually stop crying. I don't know about Tim's date, but I had a really good time on those impromptu outings.

At first, I felt guilty laughing and having fun. But then it seemed God was telling me I could be happy in spite of such deep sorrow. I later learned that most people feel this way. We think we must act like what we feel other people expect of us. I soon learned that the only person I had to please now, or care what they thought of me, was God. I knew He stood ready to help me to please Him.

I was pondering how I could teach my boys how to obey the Lord and trust him too. Besides our devotions together, I knew I must be a disciplinarian, which I was not. Michael had done something wrong, and we both knew his daddy would have spanked him. So off we went to his bedroom, and I took the paddle, and he bent over. I whacked with all my might, but he appeared to feel nothing. I just was not strong enough physically to be effective.

"Mom," he said, looking me directly in the eye, "you will never have to do that again."

Sure enough, I never did have to do that again. I was so thankful. I did find other ways to discipline, however, as perfection was not in the genes of any of the boys.

Now the boys were getting too old for spankings, so I had to get my point across some other way. This was the era when the boys were wearing their hair longer than mine. An idea came to me. So when the need for discipline came, I reached over and pulled their hair. There was one problem with this: they were runners, and when they knew discipline was needed, they would take off around the house. The design of the house was such that you could go in a circle, which they did. I began to laugh, and all benefits of the discipline went out the window. Sitting in the big chair to get my breath, I said, "Anyway, you know you shouldn't have done that, and please do not do that again."

They did get the point.

I encouraged the boys to beat a towel on the bathtub to vent their anger and frustration. Tom wore out the most towels.

We always left notes for one another so we would know where everyone was and when they would be back. This worked very well. One day, Michael decided he would run away but dutifully left us a note telling us where he was going and when he would be back. The only trouble was, his note said he was going to California and would be back when he made a lot of money. He borrowed his brother's bike, then left it at a deserted school and hitchhiked to the coast and on down the coast toward California.

Meanwhile, I had called the police and sat and waited. All night, I talked with the Lord and reminded Him of his promise to John to help me raise the boys. The thought of my young lad out there in the dark, alone, was very scary to me. The next day before breakfast, the phone rang. With fear and trembling, I lifted the receiver, not knowing if it was the police or Michael.

"Can you come get me, please? I am across the street from a grocery store in Bandon."

Now, Bandon is pretty close to the California border, so he certainly did get very close to his goal. Tom had not left for school yet, and I asked him to come with me for company to help keep me awake, as I had not slept all night and now faced a fourteen-hour drive, seven hours each way. I wondered how he had made it so far. My eyes wanted to go shut, as that was a very long trip in spite of Tom's help keeping me awake. The drive down the coast was beautiful, but oh, so full of curves. We finally reached the outskirts of Bandon and then began the search for a blond-headed kid.

"There he is, Mom."

Tom had spotted him leaning against a tree. He spotted us too and hopped in the back seat quicker than a wink. He muttered an "I'm sorry" and "Thanks."

Then he fell asleep before we could even ask any questions.

During the hours on the way home, I thought, *Now, how do I handle this?*

After we both had had enough sleep, we sat and talked about what was bothering him and why he felt he needed to get away. It must have worked, as he never ran away again. I do not know how his father would have punished him. I just had to do the best I could.

It was so helpful that Tim went to a Youth Crusade for Christ where they emphasized obeying your parents even if you felt they were wrong. They told them that God would take care of the situation. He instructed his younger brothers this way also, and it made my job so much easier.

Not long after my fortieth birthday, I received a call at work. My grandmother, who was living in a nursing home, was near death. I knew I must go to her. I was still crying and finding it hard to breathe whenever I heard a siren, so I wasn't sure if

I was strong enough to watch my grandmother die. I told my boss that I must go and headed out to the nursing home.

Now, the nursing home was close to the junior high where the boys went to school. They visited Grandma after school almost every night. They were so kind to do this. I stopped to see her after work. She always said she wanted to live to be one hundred, and so when she thought she was one hundred, she just stopped eating.

I drove in the parking lot, and it was full. I had to park a long way away. That would prove to be bad news. I prayed my way all the way to the building and down the long hall. I dreaded what I would see. Grandma was still alive, and she talked to me.

"Now I will get to go to heaven and see Grandpa. I don't like it that he has been up in heaven with Bertha all this time."

Grandpa's first wife had died before I was born. The only grandma I knew was this one. She was blind due to poor cataract surgery way back when they first started operating to remove them. She told me, "I saw Grandpa standing in the door just this morning."

Grandma's worries made me laugh. She was jealous. I knew that Grandpa and Bertha both would be there to greet her. We talked about heaven, and then in the middle of a sentence, I heard that awful gasping for breath I had heard before. I was holding Grandma when she stopped breathing and rapidly began to get cold. I called for the nurse and left.

As I stumbled out of the room, the gasping for breath

stayed with me, and I hurried to the car. As I approached the car, I knew something was not right. My back left tire was flat. Well, I would just get out the wrench and wrench off the lug nuts. I knew how to change a tire. My dad insisted that I know how before I could drive a car. But those lug nuts wouldn't budge for me. I gave it all my strength, and still they wouldn't budge an inch. I remembered that the last time I had to have a tire fixed, the tire shop had used a machine to put them on, and they were too tight for me. Now what do I do? It's at times like this one needs more than one head, if mine is the one. I sat on the grass and just bawled.

"Maybe if I hadn't had to park so far away, someone would see me and help," I moaned.

After a while, I went back to the nursing home and called Tim. He came and helped. I was thankful for muscles on my boy, as I was soon on my way. I headed back to work, but found myself at the park by the river instead. I cried and cried until I was so weak. Somehow, I managed to get back to work and finish the day.

My mother's brother and sisters decided to give me Grandma's ring. I had my old wedding ring's stones and her stones made into a beautiful ring that I wear on my right hand. It is a joy to look at it and a sweet remembrance of my grandparents.

Soon after Grandma's death, Mike and I were going through an intersection, and like a streak of lightning, a truck ran a red light. It came within inches of hitting us. We would have surely both died. Mike calmly said, almost disappointedly, "We almost got to see Dad, didn't we?"

Yes, John had taken the fear of death away for us all.

It wasn't long after that that death could have come to me as I was traveling up near Seattle on a multi-lane highway. Looking in my rearview mirror and seeing no one, I was about to change lanes when a voice said very distinctly, "Joanne."

I jerked back into my old lane as a car sped by right where I would have been. He must have come from two lanes over. I never have my radio on in the car, so when I heard a voice calling my name out loud, I was startled into action and did not question it. I thought, *How often God has to do for us what we can't do for ourselves.*

Another time, God did for me what I could not do for myself. I was returning from Portland after working all day there. I was tired beyond belief. This was before cruise control, so I had to keep my foot on the gas pedal all the time. I was trying to get home to my boys.

"God, please drive home for me. I have got to rest," I pleaded.

I felt that He agreed. So I rested my foot aside the pedal in a comfortable position, and God (or His angel) drove. Well, I soon noticed that He was not going over the speed limit at all. Now, I was anxious to get home, and so I put my foot back on the gas pedal and pushed on it in an attempt to speed up some. The car would not go any faster than the speed limit. I pushed it clear to the floor; still no results. Then a voice in my mind said, "Did you not ask Me to drive?"

"Yes, Lord. I am sorry. Thank You."

I laughed to myself; *I should have known He wouldn't go over the speed limit.*

"The phone is for you, Mom," my eldest boy announced. I took the receiver and heard the voice of our state regional minister on the other end asking if I would like to help get a new church group started in a section of Eugene.

Now, that was exciting to me, and "Yes," I responded, "I certainly would."

The area was not over thirty minutes away, so it would be easy to attend meetings, which I did. Such a blessing it was for me. The state organization must have felt the same way, as they gave me a citation, which I put up on the wall. It read: "In grateful recognition for distinguished leadership in Christian service. Joanne has been an effective builder of the Kingdom of God in Oregon through personal sacrifice and Christian dedication."

That was so nice of the Lord to let me help in his kingdom building. What would come next? I wondered.

Chapter 5
THE IDAHO TRIP

John's mother died a few months after he did. The funeral was to be held in Meridian, Idaho, where John was raised. Now, John had showed me her will, and I knew his part of the inheritance was to go to his boys.

"When they sell the farm, my share should more than pay for the boys' college. You won't have to worry about that," he had informed me.

So I thought it best the boys and I go to the funeral. It was just the next state over, and we could make it over there in a day.

The morning that we left, I read in my devotions John 14:27, "I am leaving you with a gift, peace of mind, so don't be troubled or afraid."

We had such a fun trip over, singing the songs about

Idaho that John had taught us. We arrived without mishap in Meridian and got a motel. That's when the first shock came.

As we sat down to dinner in the motel, Tom observed, "Everyone but us is wearing a gun in here."

We all looked around, and it was true.

"You can't have a concealed weapon, but it's okay to wear one in plain sight," I quietly let him know.

We were not used to that, and it made us a little uneasy. It gave the boys an idea. The prices in the motel café were too high for us, so we decided after that to eat across the street at McDonald's. We walked across the parking lot the next morning for breakfast, and I noticed the boys were surrounding me.

"Fellas, what are you doing?"

"This is tough country, so we are your bodyguards. You are a lady of importance."

Sure enough, one was ahead, and the other two were on either side of me. They all marched together, looking to the right and left. They could have pulled it off nicely, only the "lady of importance" found it very funny and started laughing.

"Mother, you are spoiling the whole effect," they complained.

We had such a good time together, but the good time ended at the funeral parlor door.

It was not hard to find the funeral parlor, as the town was so small. But first, we went by the rodeo grounds where

John had taken me to my first rodeo. It brought back really good memories, which I shared with the boys. Being in his hometown brought back so many memories that I was having a hard time keeping the tears from tumbling all over my face. It didn't help any when we entered the funeral parlor and no one greeted us. We signed the register and found a seat. (We were not asked to sit back with the family.)

After the short service, we got up and slowly left. Again, no one came over to us to say hello. I assumed his brother and sister were sitting wherever they put the family (out of sight). It gave me a creepy feeling. I was more than happy to get on the road home, but first, I wanted to go see the old farm. I was relieved to see it had been sold, so I waited a month and then called John's sister about the will and the boys' part of the inheritance. She simply said, "There is no money" and slammed the receiver down.

So much for their college education, I thought. I was not going to fight it. That would have to be another job for God and the boys to work out. None of the three was at all lazy, and they worked very hard and saved their money better than I did. I knew God would help them reach their goals, and He did.

Chapter 6
HOW STUPID CAN YOU BE? (ON A SCALE OF ONE TO TEN, A TEN?)

Soon after John's mother died, I heard about a dress shop for sale in a mall close to our house. I was certified as an optician now, so I decided to buy it and combine clothes and glasses. I would call it "The Fashion Place." Mike Gilbert, the lab tech I had worked with at my old job, made me a beautiful sign for the front of the store. You could see the sign from way down the hall. It had a very fashionable lady on one side of the sign cut out of wood and painted and a pair of beautiful glasses on the other with the lettering in the middle. The three-dimensional sign was a real eye-catcher. That was so kind of him, and I was most grateful. John had been his pastor and married Mike and his sweet wife Cara.

Knowing the optical sales reps really helped me. I ordered my frames and displays without a problem. My friend Ray from the optical lab in Portland helped me get the spendy equipment that I needed. I was especially grateful for two very rare Tura standing mirrors. I decorated the window with a latticework board with eyeglass frames hanging from it.

I was getting very excited when I was called into the mall office to sign a lease. I read it over, and it said I had to be open on Sundays. *Well, there goes a fine idea to be independent and maybe get some money for my boys' college,* I thought. I smiled at the manager of the mall, handed him back the contract, and started to get up as I told him I would not open on Sunday.

"But you have to keep the same hours as the mall. Just get someone to work for you." He sighed impatiently, thinking he had solved the problem.

"No, I wouldn't want to be the cause of someone missing out on church. I'm sorry. I really would have liked to open my own shop." I sadly gathered up my things and started out the door.

"Wait, maybe we can make an exception," he yelled after me.

I almost beat him back to my seat. They did make an exception, and I began planning the decor of my shop.

My shop was to combine clothes and women's eyewear. I would coordinate the glasses with the outfits. I knew nothing of buying clothes, but I was confident I could catch on. As I wanted high-end clothes that no one else was carrying, I scouted out some high-end clothing stores in nearby towns for the brands they carried. It was so much fun. Then I discovered the clothing industry had shows. Now, that was really going to be fun and dangerous too, I discovered. The first show was in Texas, so off on the plane I went. I felt like Little Miss Independent.

I calculated my budget carefully and flew home happy as could be with my purchases. Later, when the package arrived, it came with a little, deadly surprise.

It was not difficult to purchase the eyewear frames, as I was used to that and felt my former boss, Bill Gilbert, had schooled me well in this aspect of the business. I had also learned a lot about account receivables there.

"We'll need molly bolts if these racks are to stay up," my friend told me as he hammered in my clothing racks on the wall.

"Oh, everything is looking so nice, and I am breathing a sigh of relief as we open tomorrow," I gratefully told my helpers.

That night, I had invited my parents down from Bellingham, Washington, and also invited lots of Christian friends over to the Shoppe to ask God's blessing on it. I had planned a ceremony of songs, scriptures, poems, and prayers to dedicate it to the Lord. My three boys were there for support. My mother sang, and my father read the scripture. I was very pleased and went home very tired, so I slept well.

The next day, I rushed down to the shop, and upon entering, I gasped! All the racks on the wall had fallen down, crushing the newly pressed beautiful dresses.

Now, I had been told "It pays to advertise," and I had budgeted for that. We were well-advertised, so I was not surprised to find that when opening time came, many ladies were waiting outside the door. *This is going to be great,* I thought.

I called for help to a friend, and he brought some more friends, and before opening time, the dresses were back up on the wall again. The first disaster was lived through, but more were to come.

I was happily ringing up a sale when a lady in the back began to scream.

"Snake! *Snake!* Help! Help!" I cautiously ran to the back where she was. My eye caught a rapidly moving object heading into the baseboards. We all cleared the shop, and I closed the doors.

I ran over to the neighboring store, and the gentleman came over and searched my store but found nothing. I was not going to stay in there with a snake, so I closed for the day. That night, Tim went down to the shop and pulled off all the baseboards to find the snake. A pet shop owner came over to help. He had the proper equipment. When he caught the little critter, it was identified as a poisonous snake from Texas.

"It must have come in with your box of clothes that you just opened from Texas, Mom," Tim informed me that night.

"That is too scary for me to even think about. What if it had bitten that lady?" From then on, we looked the clothes over very carefully before we put them on a rack to sell.

Business was good, but the ladies wanted to bring their husbands in for glasses also, so I added a line for men. Then they wanted glasses for their children, so I added a line of children's frames. Business was really getting good. I was so busy I couldn't find time to eat, so my boys fixed and brought supper to me many a night and then watched the store while I ate. They took turns doing their homework at the store to keep me company (and safe) too. They were my angels!

Tim, who had a job, used his money to buy us a microwave oven. What a time-saver that proved to be. They learned to cook with it, too, but only after a few eggs exploded in it and had to be cleaned up "before Mother gets home."

A smart-looking woman came in to pick up her glasses one day and said very emphatically, "These are not the frames I chose. You mixed them up. I don't want these!"

Now, she and I knew that this was not possible, as I write down the name, size, color, etc., of the frame and drop it in its own tray. It gets double-checked as it leaves for the lab and when it comes back from the lab, and I check it out. She took them off and squinted to see them, and I knew what the problem was. Her eyesight was so poor she couldn't see what she was getting or how she looked in them.

"Grandpa, I need a video camera to take pictures of my patients so they can see what they look like in their glasses. They can put on their old glasses and look at my video of them and choose which pair they like best. We can narrow the choice down to three so it won't take so long. That way, they can see it from the side view too. I will advertise that I am the only one that has this feature. It will get me more customers and help those who have such weak eyes as well. Want to help out?" I approached my grandpa with a smile.

Now, if you knew my grandpa, you'd know the answer. I happily went video hunting. We had an old TV that would work for the screen. After that, there never was a complaint that "someone switched my glasses! I didn't order *these* frames." The video idea did bring in lots more families too.

Cataract surgery was in the infant stages, and in order for the patients to see, they had to wear bubble-like lenses. They were not at all attractive, especially if they wanted big frames, and big frames were in style. I knew the smaller the frame, the more attractive it would look and the better vision the patient would have. It took all my persuasive powers to get this across, but when I did, the results were great. They would tell their friends, and my costumer base grew and grew.

A real cowgirl came strolling in one day, cowboy boots and all.

"My secretary just bought a pair of glasses from you, and she said you helped her fit the shape of the glasses to her facial features. They really look good on her, so I flew down to get me a pair. Will you help me too?"

She had flown her private plane down from Montana. While she was there, I helped her select six pairs. She ordered regular ones, reading ones, and sunglasses. She left happy.

"When I come back to pick them up, I might get some more," she said.

Well, when she came back, she brought a friend, and her friend bought several pairs also. During the year I had the shop, she flew down several times and brought her friends. I was very flattered.

Now, I am by nature a trusting soul, so I really got caught off-guard one afternoon. Two little old ladies came in about the time I finished preparing my bank bag. One came up to the counter, and the other went back to look at a dress.

"Does this come in my size?" she softly asked. I tucked the bank bag out of sight (alas, not out of reach, apparently) and went back to help her. When I got halfway back, she said, "Oh well, I'll be back," and she quickly left. I went back to the desk and started to pick up my bank bag, and it was gone. I couldn't believe those sweet-looking little old ladies had heisted my bank bag. It had a padlock on it, so I figured they'd have to take it to their home to saw it off.

"I've just been robbed!" I excitedly yelled into the phone to the police. They came right out. The police looked all around the mall for the ladies and/or the bank bag. Nothing! Later on that evening, the phone rang.

"We have your bag. The lock is still on it. We found it in a trashcan out back. They probably thought they couldn't get it open so just tossed it. Or maybe they saw us and got scared and tossed it."

I was so grateful!

As my customer base grew, it became obvious that I would need more help. Now, I had a very fun, close friend from church, Hazel, that was also in the optical business. One evening as her husband was busy fixing my garbage disposal, I asked her if she would consider joining me.

"I have always wanted to work with brides and sell a package deal of gown and consulting," Hazel informed me. It sounded great to me. Her husband made the back corner of the shop into a bridal salon. Again, we advertised, and her business took off. Each of us helped the other.

Her bridal shows for buying gowns were at the same clothing shows that I had to go to. This would be fun! We booked our room at a cheap hotel in Seattle, as close as possible to the trade center where the show would be held. We then closed our own shop with a sign saying that we were on a buying trip, hopped in my car, and were off to Seattle. After settling in at the hotel, we decided we were hungry and began walking, looking for a place to have supper.

"Hey, there's a restaurant on the top floor of that building. Let's try it."

Off we ran and came laughing and huffing and puffing up to the maître d'.

"There will be a forty-five-minute wait," she said, looking at us rather coldly.

"I think they are trying to discourage us from eating here," Hazel whispered with a giggle.

"I think she has mistaken us for ladies of the night," I laughed.

"As there isn't any other restaurant nearby and we have nothing else to do, let's just wait."

So we settled in some comfortable chairs and began to chit-chat. The time just sped by.

"Oh my, it's almost eleven o'clock; don't you have a place for us yet?" Hazel asked.

We finally got seated. The menu was a shock, but we were able to find some interesting item and ordered it, not knowing what it was. It turned out to taste very good, but we never knew what we were eating. Perhaps that was best. It was after midnight as we stepped outside the building, and no taxi was in sight.

"We are only six blocks away from out hotel. Let's just run for it," Hazel bravely suggested.

Now, having grown up in Washington State, I was familiar with Seattle and knew the city had some dangerous parts of town, and we were in one of them. I hated to put the Lord to the test, but what else were we to do? So, bravely, we started off. We had gone only a few blocks when our worst fears began to come true.

"Do you hear footsteps behind us?" Hazel gasped.

"Yes! Let's run."

We pulled off our high heels and started to run, and the footsteps behind us began to run too.

"I'm praying real hard, and we're staying ahead of him so far." Hazel smiled.

Hazel and I worked out at the gym three times a week so were in very good shape and had a great deal of energy that a wino probably would not have unless he was on some sort of enhancing drug.

I saw Hazel's eyes grow large as the footsteps did indeed begin to catch up with us.

"Just two more blocks and we are there." I tried to encourage her and me too.

Then, as the footsteps just about overtook us, we saw the answer to our prayers, a most welcome sight. There on our corner stood a policeman, and he was looking at us. We heard the footsteps cross the street, and we ran up to the policeman.

"You ladies should not be out on the streets at this hour. Where are you going?"

I told him and pointed up the street to our hotel.

"Go ahead, and I'll watch you until you get there."

"He probably thinks we're streetwalkers too," Hazel muttered. "Who else would be out at this hour unescorted?"

We put back on our shoes. The cement sidewalk had put holes in our nylons, but we were safe. We walked the last block, softly singing praises and thank-you's to our God. God had indeed taken care of his foolish children, and I'm sure He hoped we had learned our lesson.

The next day, we walked to the show. Hazel ordered her

wedding gowns, and I ordered my dresses, blouses, and slacks. We talked and laughed all the way home.

A couple of weeks later, I discovered that there would be a class, just an hour away from our town, on collections.

"Hazel, do you want to go up to this meeting? We can do it without staying all night."

"Sure, let's go."

Thus, after work on the appropriate night, we took our notebooks and headed north to a motel in Salem, Oregon, where the meeting was being held. We giggled and laughed our way through the session, received our certificate, and were ready to head home when I lamented, "Hazel, I am really sleepy. I don't know if I can make it home. It is way past my bedtime."

"Not to worry," she replied. "Let's go get a Coke. The caffeine will keep you awake."

As we started to sip our Coke, Hazel sprinkled some salt in mine.

"What are you doing?"

"The salt will get the caffeine into your bloodstream faster," she said.

As we walked back to the car, I discovered that she was right. My eyes were opened wide and stayed that way. The only trouble was that they didn't want to close in slumber when I got home.

On the way home, we discussed all the methods of collection we had learned at the meeting. The time went fast—in fact, too fast, as the caffeine did not wear off. The next day, when it was time to go to work, I was just getting ready to fall asleep.

My business was fun and doing well. Hazel was very good at what she did, but I did not know how to buy clothes. The optical was carrying the store. When an opportunity came for me to go back to work at The Optical Shoppe, where I had worked before, I decided to take it. Hazel continued her business out of her home, plus worked for another doctor in town. She and I would meet after work at the spa or on the bike path and take long walks. The doctors had discovered cancer in her body and she was fighting that. She was doing really well for five years. We would celebrate each year. Then she began to have a backache. That awful stuff had come back, and she got to go see my John in heaven very quickly. I knew she was happy, but oh, how I missed her. Friends are such an important part of one's life.

Chapter 7
LIFE IS GETTING HARDER

One night, about six months after John died, I had a most vivid dream. I've been told this happens quite often to widows. In the dream, John took me out to dinner, and we began to discuss the boys.

"You have been doing a good job with them. You are doing a good job with the finances too. I'm really proud of you, honey."

That made me feel so good. We laughed and chatted, then started to leave. I headed for the restrooms, but as I started in, I felt a firm hand on my shoulder, stopping me.

"You aren't perfect, dear. That's the *men's* restroom!"

Oops! And I woke up.

When you lose a mate, you really need a good support group. There was a friendly, fun widow in our church who was such a blessing. Any time I feared a crying jag coming on, I would call her, and we would go out for hot chocolate. She always made herself available for me. Marcella listened to my tales of boyfriends and never condemned. We laughed together and cried together. She was older than I, but to me, age meant nothing, just as race didn't mean anything; it was how a person acted that caused me to relate to them or not. Our friendship would last a lifetime.

Tim, my eldest son, seemed to feel the financial burden of the family more than I was aware. I tried not to let it show but when their gym shoes cost so much and then got stolen or their jackets got stolen on a track meet outing, I was really discouraged, and it probably did show.

Tim was a hard worker. His first job was painting houses with a friend. Then a church member hired him to lay bricks or blocks for a store building. He would be able to use both of those trades later in his life. His senior year, he was able to get a job at the local hospital to help out in the emergency room. He thought he would like to be a doctor, and that would have been nice; he would have made a good one. He has such a caring spirit. God, however, had other plans for his life. The ER work would be of help in whatever he did for the rest of his life. I learned a lot too just by his sharing what went on and talking about the banged-up cases that came in. He put on casts and took them off. He would have gone into sports medicine. His pre-med training in college helped him a lot, as he coached football and wrestling for years at the high schools where he taught trigonometry and physics. Somewhere in there, he squeezed in a paper route, which was passed down to his younger brothers, one at a time.

Tim later took a job in the summer as the church janitor and also bucked hay. That was back-breaking work, so when the family he worked for didn't pay him as they promised, I was really mad. When they did finally pay him, the check bounced. That was the last straw. I was furious that anyone would do that to such a hard-working young man. He did finally get his money. The boys used to call me "Mama Bear," and for good reason. I was very protective of my "cubs" whom God was allowing me to have for a few short years. Tim's last job before college was with a trucking company, helping in the yard there. He really liked that, and the money was good.

Oh, it was so hard sending Tim off to the big city of Portland to get his higher education. He was a thoughtful son and kept in touch at least weekly if not more. I appreciated that so much. He invited us up to see him, and that helped a lot. It did worry me a little when someone showed me a picture of him repelling off a high building in Portland. I believe it was a picture taken by the police.

You only get your kids normally under your roof until they are eighteen; then you have to turn them back to God. I wondered, "Have I done all I was supposed to do to prepare him to walk with the Lord?" Time alone would tell me that.

All three boys would be married without the benefit of their earthly father. This made me very sad. When the eldest was married, I put on my pretty, long dress and was escorted to my seat in front. The seat beside me was empty.

My heart was so heavy. I tried to tell myself that if John were alive, he would be participating in the ceremony and not sitting beside me anyway. I thanked God for the many friends and family that were there to support us.

"Mom, I've got something for you!" Mike called to me as he entered the house one evening after a youth meeting. He eagerly showed me some paperwork on YWAM.

"Honey, what is YWAM?" My curiosity was up.

As I eagerly read the material, I discovered it stood for Youth With A Mission. The one Michael wanted to go on was a canal mission in Europe. The cost was too high for our budget, but we were supposed to get sponsors to pray for him and give money.

"Sounds wonderful. Let's fill out the paperwork." So we did and sent in the first of the money. The rest the Lord would have to provide through His people.

"It's here! It's here!" I heard from the front porch as Michael gathered in the mail. There were bookmarks with Michael's picture on them telling about his mission and leaflets telling about YWAM. The sponsorship campaign was about to begin. I took lots of the bookmarks to work and received contributions from everyone. It was not a hard sell. Then I took leaflets to all my friends in the church.

I had Michael write his great-grandparents and grandparents, aunts and uncles, and all on our Christmas card list. (I wanted to give God all the help I could.) I knew God could do it alone but usually prefers we do our part first.

The response was overwhelming, and Mike was assured that he could go on the mission. This was so exciting. The day finally came when we were to take Michael to the airport, not to fly out, but to catch a bus coming down from the north.

"Are you sure this is right, Michael? We are really waiting for a bus here at the airport terminal? There isn't anyone else here!"

"Mom, you always come early everywhere. Just allow some more time to pass, and then we can start to worry."

He was right, as it wasn't long before more kids and their parents joined us, so I felt a little better. I don't know if he had butterflies in his tummy, but I sure did. A hug and a kiss and off he went to Florida for training. I spent the time driving home in prayer for the success of his trip and his safety

After about a week, I eagerly watched for the mail each day in hopes of news from him. Finally, a letter arrived. The adults with them had made them write letters home. His letter informed me that his training was going well. They were going to be able to go to Disney World too; he was really excited about that. A couple of weeks later, a second letter came telling of their mission. They would ride and sleep in canoes, getting off to go into the towns to witness about Jesus and to hand out pamphlets. He was able to lead many young people to the Lord.

While he was disembarking (jumping off the canal boat onto shore), his wallet fell into the canal. All his money was in it. He tried to get it, but found that was impossible. He would have to figure something out for food. His fellow canal buddies came through for him. He did come home thinner than he left, but not too bad.

After their mission, they were sent to a debriefing time in a Scottish castle. He was impressed with the hundreds of bagpipes and the many, many, lights. Before he came home, he was able to buy a beautiful English china tea set for me. He held it on his lap on the plane all the way home. That was so thoughtful of him. He knew I liked things like that.

They had led two hundred young people to commit their lives to the Lord. He had learned how not to be bashful about talking to people about Jesus. I was so happy he was able to have that experience.

The following Christmas, Michael eagerly volunteered to go back down to "Boot Camp" to work. (He also got to go to Disney World by doing this.)

Chapter 8
CONVENTION SURPRISE

It was fall, and the annual National Optical Convention was coming up. I knew I needed to attend to keep up my accreditations, but where would the money come from? I was a recently widowed lady raising three young boys on a shoestring. *Ahh!* I thought. *When I closed my optical shop, I kept my Tura mirrors.* They were beautiful mirrors and of excellent quality, with a magnifying side and a regular side, two feet high, gold-encased. I knew they were very valuable now, as the company was no longer making them. I just hated to part with them, as I hoped to have my own shop again; however, my present boss wanted to buy them.

A gentleman friend from one of the optical labs had given the mirrors to me. He had since been murdered. He had walked in on a robbery, his company told me. I thought about it and decided that the Lord had given them to me (using Ray) in the first place, and if I had another shop, He would provide me two more then. (And He did.) So a deal was made, and my airfare and convention enrollment expenses were taken care of. But I still had to sell something else to pay for my hotel and food.

I sadly headed for a pawnshop in a bad part of town. Slowly, I got out of the car and began dragging my deceased husband's golf bag full of his precious clubs into the pawnshop. There, shining so brightly, was the gold-colored putter we had given him for Father's Day one year. Next, I dug in my purse and took out his gold wedding band. With tears in my eyes, I made the transaction and left with enough money, if I was careful, for the motel and food.

This had better be a mighty good convention, I sobbed as I stumbled into my old car.

A few days later, I was at the airport looking around for other opticians who might be flying to Long Beach, California, for the convention. Usually, there were several of us that went, but no luck this time. I would have to brave my airplane ride alone. I had flown the equivalent of around the world five times, but my fear of flying never diminished. Thankfully, the flight went without mishap, and we were soon taxiing in to the Long Beach airport. After I found my luggage, I was able to share a ride into the city. What a long way from the airport the city was. We got off at the convention center, and

I managed to pick a bus that went right to my motel. I noticed it was a long, long way from the convention center.

That's why it's so cheap, I thought as I lugged my luggage to the entrance. *Lord,* I prayed, glancing heavenward, *looks like I am really going to need your protection this time. This doesn't look very safe.* I would be coming home alone late at night too. I didn't want to even think about it.

The next day, the sun was shining, and I felt good as I waited at the bus stop. A nice-looking gentleman walked up and asked permission to sit beside me on the bus bench. We got to talking. He was also going to the convention. He was a publisher of optical newsletters and publications. We seemed to really hit it off. His wife had died last year, he said, and he missed her very much. He informed me he was a Christian. When we left, he asked to meet me for supper after my last class.

How bad could he be? I thought. *His name is John, the same as my late, beloved husband.* So I happily agreed to a supper date with this new man named John.

I breezed through my classes and could hardly wait for five o'clock to come.

"I saw an interesting place to eat today while I was taking a walk," said John. "Want to try it?"

Of course I did, and off we went walking together. Now, it was a good thing I was used to being in my high heels all day at work, as we were walking quite a ways.

"I know it was here somewhere," he apologized to me.

"Is that it under that building? That looks interesting!"

"You found it! Let's go!"

As I sat at the table staring at the menu, I obviously looked troubled.

"Is something wrong?" he inquired gently.

"I'm sorry; I just don't understand the words on this menu. I think I am out of my league." I smiled at him. (There were words on the menu that I couldn't even pronounce.)

"Would you mind if I ordered for you? I'd like to do that. I'll order something simple, I promise."

The meal came, and it was scrumptious. We were having a wonderful evening. As we left the restaurant I said, "I hope you know how to get back to our bus stop. I sure don't."

"I wanted a motel closer to the convention center, so I moved up to this motel." He beamed at me.

We had just arrived at a luxurious motel right beside the convention center. My heart sank. I knew even if they had a vacant room, I could not afford it. I was beginning to like this guy, and my motel was way out in the sticks.

Then he dropped a bombshell! He took me by my shoulders and, squaring me up with him so he could look me square in the eye, he began to speak.

"I moved you, too. Our rooms are right next to each other by the pool."

My head was swimming. *How could he get in and get my*

stuff? This just doesn't seem real. Well, at least he was kind enough to get two rooms, not just one for the two of us.

"Let's go swimming; it's a beautiful night," he meekly suggested as he handed me my room key.

"Meet you in the pool in fifteen minutes."

Stunned, I unlocked my room and went inside. I changed to my bathing suit and headed the few steps to the pool. The water felt ohhhh so good … He soon came out and joined me. We laughed and played like little kids. It was fun under the stars.

"Would you like anything to drink before you go to bed?" he asked as I climbed out of the pool and headed for my room.

"No, thanks! See you in the morning. I'll probably go swimming before breakfast."

My heart was racing as I went into my beautiful room and *locked the door.* I felt very safe as I had my devotions and lay smiling on my bed. I sleepily let thoughts run through my head. *Could God have sent this nice man to be of help to me at this time*? He certainly did not appear to demand or require anything of me. He had asked me to be his companion at a dinner ball on the *Queen Mary* ship in the harbor. I would be outclassed, I knew. I hadn't brought any long dress and couldn't buy one. I had brought my beautifully embroidered, red South American dress. It was far from sexy, as the neck was a turtleneck, so no chance of cleavage showing there. The length was just above the knee. *My legs are pretty enough, so that will just have to do. The best I have.*

When I was riding in from the airport, I had seen the *Queen Mary* ship and thought, *I'd like to go on that, but fat chance of that happening.* I felt like Cinderella. *God is so good,* I thought.

The sun woke me as it shone brightly through the glass wall, reflecting off the pool. I quietly put on my swimsuit and stepped out and into the pool. With easy strokes, I swam to the other end of the pool. As I made a U-turn, I saw John coming out of his room and jumping into the pool. *What a wonderful way to start the day,* I mused. After we dressed, he came knocking at my door, and we had devotions together. Then we went our separate ways to our classes.

I was very excited as I got myself dressed for the dinner ball that night. Right on time, John knocked on my door, and we were off to the limo.

As we walked out of the motel, he whispered in my ear, "You look beautiful tonight." That helped me so much, as when one feels one looks okay, one can forget about oneself and think about other people.

Another couple that we were going with was already in the limo.

"Joanne, I'd like you to meet Ruth and Jim Gooding. He is the state president of the opthamalagists in my state."

Now I knew I was outclassed. She had on a beautiful, long dress and lots of real jewelry that sparkled every time she moved. In spite of that, she and I hit it off right away.

When we were alone on the boat, she told me how popular John was with the ladies back home, how they fell all over themselves to get his attention.

"We were shocked when he told us he had invited you to this dinner. We are very pleased."

They would be even more shocked if they knew he had moved me up to a motel right next to the convention center and right next to his room. I thought it best not to mention it. They might get the wrong idea, and so far, he had been a perfect gentleman.

The evening was going so nicely. I was enjoying walking around and seeing the ship; the dinner was excellent; and as the dance floor was too crowded, we just listened to the music and visited. I felt so fortunate that none of my party smoked, as I have an allergic reaction to cigarette smoke. I always found it very difficult to answer "Yes" when asked, "Do you mind if I smoke?"

Weariness was taking over when at last they decided it was time to go back to the motel. John politely dropped me off at my door and kissed my forehead.

"See you in the pool in the morning, beautiful lady," he whispered sweetly. I looked into his eyes, smiled, and then slipped into my room and bolted the door. I fell asleep almost before my head hit the pillow.

The days passed happily and quickly, and before I knew it, it was time to leave for home. It had been a really great convention, and I had taken lots of notes. I had also earned an Elizabeth Arden fashion certificate and a Gloria Vanderbilt one to put on the wall. I had taken classes in the art of dispensing contacts and dyeing lenses for fashion. It was well worth my time and money.

Now I had to check out and head for the airport. John was going to accompany me out to the airport, but he sent word they had called a meeting he had to attend, so he could not accompany me. I was scared to check out, as I had no money and no credit card. I knew I would have to write a check. But as I went to the payout window, the lady handed me my bill, and it said "Paid in full." I could not believe it. As I turned to leave, there stood John with a big grin on his face.

"I only have a minute but had to tell you good-bye."

He hailed a taxi, *paid him*, grabbed me, and kissed me tenderly while pushing me gently into the taxi.

"I'll be in touch!" he yelled, and I was off, waving out the back window.

Riding out to the airport, I relived the past few days. It seemed like a dream, a very nice dream, but not reality. Thoughts were whirling around in my head. Would I ever hear from him again? Had he come into my life too soon after my John's death? Was he out of my league? Would I embarrass him someday because he ran around with a different class of people? Maybe there was no "class" of people if you found the right people.

After work the next day, the phone was ringing as I headed into the house. The boys weren't home yet, so I had no trouble answering it. I recognized the voice immediately.

"I'm just checking to see if you got home okay. I miss you already. Look on your calendar and see when you can fly back to visit me. I'll send you the plane tickets and put you up in a hotel. We'll have lots of fun seeing my town of Saint Louis."

That night was my businesswomen's group, so I had to hang up and get dinner started, but I promised him I would look at my calendar and get back to him soon.

At the businesswomen's meeting, everyone was talking about the national convention that was to be held the next month in Saint Louis. Wow! That would be a perfect time to go back and see John.

The next day, I called John and told him my good news. He seemed so happy.

"Don't buy any plane tickets yet until I check with my boss to see if I can get the time off."

I excitedly told my boss about the businesswomen's national meeting in Saint Louis the next month and said that as I was president of the Eugene chapter, I really needed to go. I waited as he looked sadly at me and said, "I'm sorry, Joanne, but I have to have that time off. I have planned it for a long time. You cannot go."

Now, as I still had my children at home. I could not risk losing my job, so I called John that night and informed him of my disappointing news.

"I am so sad. I would love to come see you and your town, but I cannot afford to lose my job. I know we would have a wonderful time together."

"I can easily take care of you and your family for the rest of your life. You would not have to work unless you wanted to," he informed me.

John took it that I did not want to see him. He was hurt. It was evident he had plenty of money and he was willing to share it with me if I continued our relationship. I really did not want to move my boys clear across the country. I never heard from him again, nor saw him at any future conventions. I did see the other couple that went to dinner with us on the *Queen Mary,* and they informed me John had gotten married. I knew he would, as he was a good catch. It just was not my time. I had not finished raising my boys yet.

Chapter 9
I AM HAPPY BY MYSELF, THANK YOU!

While out front in the Optical Shoppe adjusting glasses, I heard the men in the back talking about me to someone. When I went to the back to get a tool, they introduced me to the president of the University of Oregon. He was a nice-looking, tall redhead. He was divorced and needed someone to go with him to some of the university's functions he had to attend. Now, I felt very strongly about divorced men and did not want anything to do with them. They just came with too much baggage, especially if they had children. I knew how my boys felt about a stepdad, and their dad was dead. How would kids feel about a stepmom if their mom was still living? One of my fellow opticians once told me, after her husband's ex-wife was dragging him into court again, for the fifth time, "I'll shoot you on the way down the aisle if you even think about marrying a divorced man."

I quickly picked up the tool I needed and scooted out front. I deliberately stayed out front until I knew he was gone. When I came to the back again, I informed the men that I would not be the least bit interested in that redhead. Word got back to him, and he never asked me to anything. He did come into the shop and joked and teased with me some. He probably was a very nice man, I would never know.

The churches in our town took turns having a devotional for the homeless at the mission. It was our church's turn, and they asked me if I would do it.

"Sure," I replied and then began to plan it.

As I was thinking out loud about it at work the next day, my boss said, "I could come and lead songs, if you like. I've done that before."

Sounded like a good idea to me, as I couldn't play the piano and lead songs too.

Thus, after work on that night, we headed for the mission. It was not in a good part of town, and I was glad to have a big man with me. All went very well, including my talk. Afterwards, as we were having a hot chocolate, he said, "Your talk was good, but did you see all the men fidgety? They were eager to get to their meal, I think."

I really didn't think that sort of thing was my calling. I didn't volunteer, and I was never asked again. That was all right with me.

Later on that year, I could not believe what I was hearing from my boss. He had called us all to a meeting and informed us that he was in charge of the beer gardens at the Veneta Festival. It seemed he wanted us all to volunteer to work at the gardens. He needed help, he said.

One after another began to volunteer. Finally, I was the only one left who had not volunteered. He reminded me that he had helped me and now I must help him.

"Oh, no, no," I protested.

"You have to; don't you want your job?"

"I'm sorry. Do you really think that would hold up in court?"

I did not go and kept my job too.

Now, as I had no steady fellow to play tennis with or golf or go skating with, each boy would take turns being my sports companion. I wanted to learn to dance, and the Elks lodge was having classes. The boys would take turns taking me. The only problem was, as they took turns, they didn't know the steps that were learned the week before. They toughed it out, and I learned a lot. It was fun for me but not for my boys. I played golf with the eldest boy, Tim, until he got good and wanted to play with some of his own friends. I played tennis with each one until poor Mike was the only one left and had to do it all. There was no one left to share the burden of mother. He and I played tennis when the court had patches of ice on it. After slipping badly, we gave it up. I finally had to give up and go to the gym for my exercise. Not near as much fun. I missed the outdoor air.

About this time, I was going to several Christian singles groups. It is not nice to say this, but the people in the meetings I was going to all seemed like losers. They had awful attitudes.

Singles retreats netted me spiritual food, but no one of the opposite sex, even to be friendly with for more than one date.

I knew several nice singles that were fun, so I started a singles group at my house. We got a neat recently married couple to lead us. We all had such a good time bowling, eating pizza, skating, eating Mexican food, going to movies, eating Chinese food. The group grew and grew. So did I with all that eating.

Then a terrible phenomenon began to occur. They began marrying one another. Couple by couple left for the married state of bliss until I again found myself alone with the married leaders.

So much for that idea, I thought. *I didn't want to get married; I just wanted fun Christian companionship. A good stranger is hard to find,* I concluded. There surely was someone out there that would want my gorgeous body, smiling face, and all that love I had stored inside me. Solitude, the single life, or give it up. I decided I was happy as a single and would just stay that way.

Chapter 10

THE SINGLE MOM'S LIFE

The middle boy, Thomas, was ready to learn to drive. The lab tech at my work informed me that boys who learned to drive from their mothers drove "like a woman." He was implying that was pretty awful. So, after giving the boys the basics, I tried to get an elder or deacon or male friend in the church to help me out. With Tim, I just jumped right in, and off we went. He drove out in the country. He misjudged a corner, and we headed into a ditch.

"Tim, keep your foot on the gas or we will be stuck. You can just drive on up out of the ditch."

I usually fall apart after the emergency, which I did this time. That finished our afternoon session. He did a beautiful job of driving the next time out. I knew he would be a good driver, but he always fell asleep right away when we took family trips. So I worried the first time he drove on a long trip by himself. He was able to cope very nicely and did indeed turn out to be a good driver that didn't "drive like a woman," as my co-workers felt would happen.

Now it was my turn to sit next to Tom. Tom was an entirely different personality from his older brother. As I wanted the boys to know how to use a clutch, we started off with a clutch car. I should have worn a neckbrace. He was really jerky.

When I felt he was fairly safe, one of the deacons in the church offered to help. Tom drove us to church so proudly each Sunday and very quickly got his license. This was oh so helpful, as he could take himself to sport functions and activities at church and school and to his after-school and weekend jobs. What I didn't figure into the equation was that he could also go visit his girlfriend. He was very good at coming home at the allotted time, and so I didn't have to worry about him. That was a blessing.

Michael did very well when it was his turn. In fact, I soon forgot that he was just learning, and we traveled toward the California border and took a motel in California for the night, as I wasn't paying attention and he was driving so well. We had fun and a mini-vacation.

One time, this stupid mother (me) had him drive up a road in the mountains. The further we got, the worse the road got. Finally, it became one-way and seemed to be going nowhere. He had to try to turn around, which was not an easy thing to do. He did a fine job.

My boss decided he would help me teach Michael to drive.

So one night after work, he came by the house and took Michael out for a spin. When an hour passed and they had not gotten home, I became concerned. When they did finally get back and we thanked my boss, I asked Michael, "Why did you take so long? Dinner has been ready a long time."

"He fell asleep right after I took the wheel. I didn't know where I was supposed to go."

A lot of help he was to my boy.

"You poor thing! Raising three teenage boys must be awful!" people would say to me. They did not know how helpful my boys were. I taught them to do their own laundry and wash the floors (their daddy had taught them that "washing floors was man's work"). They also learned to defrost the fridge, wash the ring out of the tub, vacuum, and dust. What I didn't realize was that they also knew how to cook. When they went on hiking trips, they could cook very well. I seldom, if ever, was sick, so they didn't have to cook at home unless I was gone or they wanted to surprise me. My daughters-in-law should be grateful. (And they are.)

As the head of the house, I found that when I paid my taxes, I didn't get a break like the married folk got. I also discovered you couldn't get a credit card from department stores like Sears, Penney's, Meir and Frank's, Bond's, etc. This seemed so unfair. I found out that a lab tech where I worked made less money than I did. His house was not paid for. He had not worked at his present job as long as I had, yet he got a credit card at the very place that had turned me down. I called them up and confronted them.

"We can't issue cards to single women" was their reply. That made it very unfair. I'm glad all that changed some years later (after I was a married woman again). I still insisted on getting my cards in my name. Just a hangover thing from being mistreated as a single woman.

One of the other areas of unfairness to women that I experienced was when I had to have my car repaired or buy new tires or even try to buy a new car. I just couldn't believe it. So, although it made me mad, I finally got so I would ask an elder or deacon in the church to come with me to pick up my car after it had been repaired. Then when they told me what all "more" they needed to do, I had some backup to tell them," No thanks." They also checked to see that the work they said they did actually had been done. When I had a flat, they would often tell me two more tires were so bad I would get a flat very shortly. After male advice, I could confidently tell them, "I'll just chance it, thank you."

When my car began to wear out, I found a nice used one and decided to trade up. I knew what I could pay and had decided ahead of time not to go any higher. Now, as I have said before, buying a car for me had always been a man's job. I just picked the color. So I chose a man in the church and ask him to go with me. I took Mike with me too.

Things were going well, I thought, until they took my car

out to see what they would give me for it on the trade-in. I really didn't care what I got for my old car, just so long as the bottom line came out to what I had saved for the new car and I didn't need to borrow any money. When he came back with his report, it sounded like I had taken my life in my hands just driving down to his lot. My heart sank, and I began to condition myself for not getting the car that I had my eye on.

After running around like they do, back and forth (I wonder sometimes if they just go out and go to the bathroom and then come back and say their memorized piece), he finally was getting close to my figure.

"If you can make the bottom line come out to this amount of dollars, sir, we have a deal. If not, I am leaving. That is the amount I can spend."

"Oh, you can do a little bit more than that, I'm sure. Just add the price of the new plates, and the title."

Now, I had made a deal with the Lord that I would not spend over a certain amount, and that title and license fee made it come above that amount, So, as much as I wanted that car, I knew that if the total price came above what I had promised the Lord I would spend, that was not the car for me, and I would just have to hunt some more.

I stood up and headed for the door with the salesman following me, telling me (and everyone in earshot) how I should take the car. How I was stubborn over a few dollars, etc., etc. My friend drove me out of the parking lot, and I was in the back seat. We drove around the building to get to the exit, but we never made it to the exit, as the sales manager came running out a side door and pounded on the car window. We stopped, and I rolled down the window.

"You can have it for that price you insist on, and we will pay the title and license. Come on back in." Thus I concluded this was the car God approved of, and I got the car that turned out to be my favorite one of all time. I just had to be true to the bargain I had made with God.

Chapter 11
ARE VACATIONS FUN ALONE?

One of the ladies in our church wanted to go to Alaska on a cruise ship and share the expenses with me. The idea was very appealing. She would take her car, and we would drive to Seattle and stay in a hotel on the water right by the loading dock so we could just walk to the ship. The trip was not very expensive, so I thought I could swing it just fine. The day came to leave, and ten minutes after I hopped in her car, I knew I had made a mistake. Something was not right. She drove up part of the way to Seattle, and we got a motel. When we were waiting to eat, she began getting very nervous and started yelling at the waitress. I thought maybe she was diabetic and really did need her food, so I asked her. But no, she just wanted her food *"right now!"* She ate so fast and then was ready to go to the room. I had only taken a few bites of mine.

"Is something bothering you, Rose Ann?" I inquired.

"No, no. Just hurry up; I want to go to the room, but not alone."

This was weird. I began to feel uneasy.

When we got to our room after a nice walk, she again became very nervous and began to pace the floor. I just went to bed. About an hour later, I heard her say, "I can't sleep! What shall I do?"

Luckily, I can sleep under the most trying circumstances and was able to get back to sleep. I woke up once about three AM and found her out in the hall pacing up and down. I couldn't figure out what was wrong with her.

The next day, I drove on up to Seattle while she fidgeted in the passenger side. We pulled into our bayside hotel and parked. The room was lovely. It was right over the water. They advertised that you could fish from your room and the cook would fix it for you for supper. We just ate what someone else caught. I was almost embarrassed to go with her to supper after how she had been acting lately. I was glad when the meal was over. She went into the gift shop and bought a very expensive "man of the sea" statue. It took all her money, and from then on, she borrowed money from me for food and anything else she wanted.

"I'll pay you back when we get home," she insisted. (I never got a cent from her or for her half of the trip either. I couldn't believe it. I presented her with an itemized list of her expenses and asked for it once, and she said, "Oh yes, I do owe you some money, don't I?")

The next day, we got on the ship that headed for Victoria Island, where we would board our cruise ship. We stayed in a hotel that night and would board the next day. Again, she started acting strange. When we got to our room, I sat her down and very firmly asked, "Rose Ann, what is wrong with you? You don't usually act like this."

Then she confessed.

"I knew you were allergic to cigarette smoke, so I decided to use this time to quit smoking. I've wanted to quit for some time now."

"I didn't even know you smoked," I stuttered.

How were we to overcome this problem? She was jittery, cross, fidgety, impatient, and downright rude. Not a nice combination of traits to be around and have to spend time cooped up with in a small ship cabin. Neither could I take her smoking. Time would find its own answer.

We soon were all settled nicely in our cabin, and the ship headed out to sea.

I took my seasick pills so I could be out on deck and enjoy it. I was standing alone when a hunk of a man came alongside me and started up a conversation.

This is going to be a fun trip after all, I assured myself. It certainly was starting out nice. It seemed he was traveling on business. He was working for the FBI. Sadly, he had lost his wife less than a year ago and asked if I would join him for dinner.

"I really hate eating alone. That's the worst part of being single." He smiled and winked.

As Rose Ann was sick and didn't want to eat, I accepted his invitation. It was exciting dressing for supper. He had obtained a table right at the front of the boat where we could see everything. The sun was just setting, sprinkling lovely colors on the aqua water. When the food came, he reached for my hand, like an automatic response, then bowed his head, and we had a silent prayer.

The salmon dinner was exceptional, and we had a very enjoyable time. Afterwards, we listened to their music and watched the entertainment. He asked if he could spend time with me the next day, and I gladly replied, "I'd like that also."

He had shared so many interesting happenings with me. His life was totally different from anything I could imagine. I never watch murder mysteries or thrillers, so what he was telling me that he had been through seemed so unreal to me. I wanted to hear more. I could hardly wait for the next day to come. But the next day, Rose Ann was very sick and wanted to go home. We were stopping at a port, and she wanted to get off and fly home.

"I have to end my cruise, and already I will miss you. You seem like a very nice man," I sadly told my newfound interesting friend.

"No, *no,* no," he replied. "I have to go to Alaska, but I will be coming back through and will be driving through Eugene. Please let me call you and take you to dinner. You just can't walk out of my life!"

So that is how we left it. Rose Ann and I disembarked and flew to Vancouver, British Columbia, then on to Seattle and picked up her car and came home. What a horrible but exciting vacation. The next day, I received a bouquet of roses from him. They were beautiful, and it was fun getting the flowers. But they lasted longer than he did.

About a week later, while at work, I got a phone call.

"Your FBI man is on the phone for you," I was teased.

"I'm at the rest area just south of Portland, so should be in Eugene about the time you get off work. I'll meet you at our planned spot. Things have not gone well for me, but I'm sure it will be safe. See you soon." The receiver went dead.

Why was he whispering? I wondered. He had told me his first wife simply couldn't take the danger. I wondered if I wanted to get mixed up in this. He was a nice, Christian man, but what would my life be like with him? Well, I would not ever find out, as when I went to our designated spot to meet, he never showed up. He never called. I never heard from him again. Only God knows the rest of that story.

Chapter 12

OH NO! BACK IN THE DATING GAME!

It might be hard knowing who the Lord has planned to be your life partner, but I didn't think I had any trouble figuring out who He didn't want me to have. A pastor friend in Los Angles had an elder in his church who had been widowed for two years and wanted to get back in the dating game but just didn't know how, he informed me one day on the phone.

"I gave him your number; I hope you don't mind. He is really nice. He has no children and would love your boys. Do give him a chance, please."

So when the phone rang later on that day, I started getting acquainted with the policeman from LA. We did seem to think alike on a lot of things. I gave him my address, and we began a long-distance friendship/courtship-type relationship. We sent each other our pictures. He called every night, and we would talk and talk.

Again, I enjoyed the flowers that he sent. They made me feel so special. After a few months, he informed me he had a vacation coming up and he wanted to come up and meet me and my boys. I was excited. Then I got the call that changed everything for me. His voice seemed very strange. It was scary to me.

"I have just killed a man. He drew a gun on my partner and shot him but missed. I knew he would probably not miss the second time, so I shot him. I was not on duty but coming home to pack to come see you. I have to stay now until this is all settled. I have been on the force twenty-five years, and this is the first time I have had to kill someone."

After we hung up, I knew I did not want him to come see me or to continue our relationship. He needed to find someone else who could handle what policemen's wives have to go through. I knew I couldn't. We broke up our relationship, but maybe he was able to date locally after that and could find himself a suitable mate. I knew I wasn't the one for him.

"Joanne, I did something I hope you won't be too mad about. I have been phone-dating two men at the same time and have decided on one so gave the other one your phone number. He is a millionaire from Texas, and I think you should give him a chance. I just dumped him, so he will probably be calling you soon."

Sally, from our Christian singles group, always wanted to *help me out.*

She was right. It didn't take Bill long to call. It wasn't long until we too were exchanging photos and talking every night and I was enjoying fresh flowers at work. (During my eight years of being single, the florist shops in Eugene should have appreciated me; I certainly did appreciate them.)

Bill was about to fly up to see me when he laid a bombshell on me.

"When we get married, we will be traveling all over the world." (I hate to fly; strike one). "We will put your boys in a private school in England." (Strike two. No one takes my boys from me.) "You can visit them when we go to England." (Strike three, you're out!) "They will stay under my roof until they are ready for college."

Thus I ended the relationship with my Texas millionaire.

Now, I did not know there were so many millionaires that were widowed running around back in the seventies, but I happened on another one. This one seemed to have more possibilities. Again, it was through this same friend, Sally, from the Christian singles group.

"You'll really have a lot in common with this nice man, and he is closer. At least one of his homes is in Washington. He is going to the mission field to help out, as he is a medical doctor. I've told him about you. He is good-looking and has a lot of women after him. Give him a chance. He is going to call you."

Why should he call me, I wondered, *if he has all those other woman after him?* But call me he did, and we set up a date. I was driving up to see my parents that next weekend and would go right by his town, so we set up a luncheon date to get acquainted.

Why do I keep doing this? I asked myself. *I am perfectly happy by myself. I am learning to live without the male figure in my life.* In fact, my boys felt I was getting *too* independent. They insisted on opening my doors for me and pulling out my chair so that I would not forget that I was a "*lady!*"

When the right exit came up off the freeway, I was tempted to keep going and apologize later. It was noon, and I was hungry, so I turned the steering wheel and found myself parking at the restaurant. As I entered, a very nice, good-looking gentleman hurried up to me and introduced himself. I had told him what I would be wearing, and he knew I was a blond, so he felt pretty confident that I was the right woman.

No sooner had we sat down than a pretty lady about our age came over and asked to talk to him. She took him by his arm to pull him up off his chair. He didn't budge but very politely introduced me to her and then very firmly informed the woman that he would have to talk to her later. We were barely able to order before a second woman came up to talk to him. She pulled up a chair as if to join us. He looked at me and smiled, and he then stood up and pulled her chair out and told her sweetly that they would have to talk later. She grudgingly left, and he put her chair back. I soon lost count of how many women came up and at least touched his shoulder and smiled at him.

"You are really 'Mr. Popular.' Does this happen to you every time you go out?"

"I make it a point not to go out very often. I have another home on a lake in California and one near Chicago. We could meet there, and it would be more private."

"This will have to do for now," I informed him.

He had a good sense of humor, and the luncheon was going nicely, in spite of the interruption by good-looking women. There was one thing that I could not handle and felt I could not live with the rest of my life. When he went to eat, he would pick up his food and then jerk it ninety miles an hour into his mouth.

How could he get so old and educated in life and not have broken such an awful habit? I wondered. *I would soon have the jerks just watching him,* I thought.

When I got to my parents', I was telling my mother, and she suggested, "You could just eat in separate rooms."

Even though he was going to a mission hospital on an island that spoke Spanish, so I wouldn't have to learn a new language, I knew he and I would not work out. Some other gal would probably gladly put up with his jerky eating for his million bucks. Happy relationships to me were far more important than cold money, so I stopped our relationship so he could get on with one of his many admirers. I did leave him my trademark cinnamon rolls.

Chapter 13
LIFE IS NOT FAIR

"Boys, I have some bad news. Your daddy's sister's son, Larry, is coming over from Idaho to take our big claw-legged oak table back to 'Sis,' and the rolltop desk as well. She also wants the record player. Remember, Daddy said if his family came for the furniture, to let them have it. Larry and his sister Sally Ann had lived with us while we were pastoring in Elma, Washington, before you were born."

"But, Mom, didn't we pay Grandma for them?"

"Yes, but that doesn't seem to matter to your daddy's sister. She wants them and feels we should give them up."

"Will she pay for them?" Tom asked.

"No, honey, they will just come with a U-Haul and take them away."

The boys didn't like this at all, and neither did I.

"That's just not fair," they complained.

"I agree with you, but life is not always fair," I sighed.

Well, I had taken the old phonograph and put red velvet on the speaker part and polished it all up. We had some old, old thick records that we loved to listen to and often cranked it up.

I'm just going to hide the phonograph at a friend's house, I thought to myself.

So that very evening, it disappeared out our front door to visit a friend until danger had passed. I was so glad that I had done that and so glad that they never asked about it. I knew she wasn't going to enjoy it but just sell it for lots of money. I felt that was what she was going to do with the table, chairs, and rolltop desk too. She did that very thing, for Hazel, my dear friend, found the rolltop desk in an antique shop in Idaho. Hazel knew that one of the handles on a drawer was different from the others, plus there was a chip on the left side in the back. Sure enough, the one Hazel found was just like mine. She called me up and wanted to know if I wanted her to buy it for me.

"Oh Hazel, how much is it?"

My heart sank when she told me. I could not justify spending that much money, so I assigned that piece of furniture to a memory-only status.

The table was very heavy, and I knew the boys did not want to help carry it out when they came to pick it up, but they did. Many a meal had been served off of that table to family and strangers alike. I shed my tears, and we carried on with life.

Tim had been invited to go skiing with some church folk, and away he went. He had a wonderful time and really got hooked on the fun sport. However, he did not have skis, nor boots or poles. As money was so tight and I wished to get them for him for Christmas, I knew the only way possible would be to ask the other two boys if they would sacrifice their Christmas wish lists for Tim. They eagerly said yes. I thanked God for such selfless boys. That Christmas, Tim got his needed skis, boots, and poles. This non-skier mom didn't realize gloves were needed too. After he froze his fingers, some friends loaned him some of their gloves, and he was a happy skier.

I took the children out to eat once in a while so they would learn manners and feel comfortable dining in places other than McDonald's. It was at one such occasion that Tom stepped on a package of ketchup and it squirted on his big brother's pant leg. This did not go over well with his big brother. A word fight started, and I tried in vain to calm it down and stop it. Finally, in desperation, I threatened to "dance on the table" if they didn't stop. There was deathly silence. Tim told Tom, "She'll do it, too." I was glad I didn't have to follow through with that threat, but Tim was right—I would have done it.

When I came home from work one evening, I noticed all three boys were very quiet and busy in Tom's room. I started to open his door, and they all yelled, "Don't come in, Mom."

As it was not near a holiday or my birthday, I couldn't imagine what they all would be doing together that would not include me. I would later be included but wish I wasn't.

I left them alone and decided I'd find out later what was going on. I fixed supper, and when we were eating, I brought up the subject again.

"You really don't want to know, Mom. Trust us on this one."

"Someone tell me, please. Tom, it was your room, so you please tell me."

"I volunteered to keep the class scorpion and care for it. I have had no problems until today," he finally volunteered. Oh, dear me. I wondered how long I had been living in the same house with a scorpion.

"Today it got out, and we can't find it," he continued.

"How are we going to be able to sleep with a live scorpion running around somewhere in the house?" I inquired.

After the supper dishes were done, we all resumed the search for the elusive scorpion. It had found a spot out of sight and was not going to make its presence known. Tom felt badly that he had lost the class scorpion. I felt nervous about going to bed with its whereabouts still unknown. We all slept that night and the nights to follow too, as we never did find it. When we sold the house, the scorpion went with the deal.

Soon after that, a friend from church came up to me and pleaded, "Please, Joanne, go with me to the junior college and take this class. I don't want to go alone. It will be good exercise and lots of fun."

"What class?"

"The belly dancing class."

"You've got to be kidding! We're in our forties. I can't bend and twist like I used to in my twenties. We'll hurt ourselves."

After a few seconds' thought, I concluded that it just might be fun, and besides, who would believe me anyway? So off we went Tuesdays and Thursdays to the college. The first night, we showed up at class a little scared. We should have been.

"I don't think anyone here is even in their thirties but us *'old'* ladies," I whispered in my friend's ear.

The class began, and the teacher started out easy. We began to know the other students and bonded right away. We sat in a circle and had to tell what occupation we were going into or were in. I really didn't want to say "minister's wife," and I really wasn't that anymore. I did share with them that I was recently widowed and my husband that died was a minister. Then we were asked, "Why are you taking this class?"

I said, "if I ever marry again, I'd love to surprise the heck out of my new husband." (And I did.) It was worth it!

The teacher told us where to go to buy our supplies, castanets, etc. While buying them later in the week, we saw our fellow students, and they shouted clear across the store to us. Then when I was at the grocery store, one student came up to me, gave me a big hug, and introduced me to her boyfriend. We had been accepted.

I wanted to go see a belly dancer perform, but where and how would this be possible? I approached the gentleman that I was going out with about it. To my surprise, this Baptist gentleman knew where there was a restaurant that had a belly dancer. It was a hundred miles away in Portland. He was willing to take me, so off we went. On the way up, I said, "This is exciting and fun." But I began to feel ill at ease as we drove into the seedy part of Portland and parked. I wondered if his Cadillac would have any hubcaps on it or even if a tire might be missing when we came back.

To my delight, the restaurant was nice; we had a lovely meal. The fellow patrons were not seedy-looking but looked just like us. The belly dancer was beautiful and began to dance just as I had been taught. I recognized her steps and moves. I was glad I had come.

The next belly dance I went to was with the whole class. The gals were very modest, and it was fun. I was sorry to have the class come to a close. I would miss our young friends. I could now sway and swivel and move my head side to side like a cobra. I had never imagined that I could do that. I tucked all my belly dancing things in a box in the closet, never to see the light of day for many a year. I have never regretted taking the class. It was an adventure indeed.

Chapter 14
A SPECIAL GIFT

"Joanne, I want to talk to you."

I was at work heading down the hall to the lunch room and heard my name being called. I stopped and waited for the doctor to catch up with me. I usually tried not to have much to do with this doctor, as he was single and a little older than I was, and I knew he was dating a lot. I had heard (from one of the women in our office that had dated him) that he had a boa in his bedroom. My dislike of snakes made him off-limits to me. (Not that I was planning on going in his bedroom, you understand.) I had also heard that one of his dates came to his house, and when he opened the door, she threw open her coat and had nothing on and then said, "What you see is what you get." He must not have liked what he saw, as he didn't date her for very long.

"You need a dog at your house with your three boys. My

Labrador just had puppies and I'll give you one if you want. I'll deliver it to you when they are weaned." That was very thoughtful of him. I accepted gratefully.

I hadn't even thought about a dog, but it did sound like a good idea. Then when the boys were gone, he would be a nice companion for me and a nice watchdog.

Thus our household gained a very expensive puppy that we all fell in love with. His paws were so big for the rest of him; I knew that was a clue as to how big he would grow. Now I would have to add dog chow to my grocery list. As John's uncle, who had sent him to college, owned the Purina Chow food store in Nampa, I felt obligated to buy Purina. It must have been good, for the dog had lots of pep and stayed healthy.

Everyone told us how smart this breed of dog was. I didn't want a dog smarter than me. I think it was a close match, because Sam was smart. We'd open the sliding glass door, and he would peek in but never step foot in the house until someone called his name. Then he would march directly to the big chair and lie down alongside it. He never offered to go elsewhere in the house unless one of the boys called him from a bedroom. Then he would go directly there, never deviating. He was a wonderful dog and grew up to be beautiful.

After the two older boys had gone to college and Mike and I were home alone, we had a tragedy. I came home from work while Mike was still at track practice. I opened the screen door and called "Sam," but no Sam came. I ran to the neighbors to see if they knew anything.

"Two men came this afternoon and went into the back yard. They left carrying Sam. We thought it was strange."

We called the police but never did get Sam back. He was a valuable dog, and someone wanted to cash in on him. Sam was the last dog that we had. We moved shortly after that.

"Mom," the middle boy, Tom, addressed me after supper one night while we were clearing up the dishes. "Our junior high choir is singing tomorrow in the assembly, and the parents are invited."

"Thanks, son, I'll see what I can do."

The next day, I skipped out of work just in time to race over to the junior high (which was in the next town) and made it just in time to hear the choir director announce, "Tom King will be singing the solo in this number." Wow!

I settled back and wondered what I was going to hear. I had not heard Tom sing very much by himself. I was astonished as my little boy threw back his head and let it roll out. I could not believe it. What a beautiful voice God had given him. *Oh, how I wish his daddy could be here to hear this,* I thought. I knew John heard him, but he and I didn't get to share it together. This being a single parent was not fun. Not only did I not have his and her parenting skills, but I also didn't have anyone to share the joys with either, and there would be many a joy with all three boys as they grew and accomplished many things to be proud of. I sat alone for each one as they graduated. I had to rely on Philippians 1:6: "Being confident of this, that he who began a good work in you will carry it on to completion until the day of Christ Jesus." I wanted their daddy there so badly.

When the first grandchild came, I wanted a grandpa there with me. I had fun playing with our grandkids, but it would have been twice as much fun if John had been there to share with us.

Tom was growing up, and I knew he would soon be leaving the house for his own lodging while going to college. He had fixed up his room so nicely for himself. He had a strobe light that flashed so brilliantly that it kept me out most of the time. His senior year, he was gone a lot at Janine's house for dinner or to play or whatever excuse he could find to be there. He especially enjoyed visiting in two homes of our church folk and eating that mama's food. One mama told me she enjoyed making him a mixing bowl full of mashed potatoes and watching him eat them. Tom was very skinny but could finish the whole bowl when encouraged. One family even took him on their vacation with them. That was so nice. They are now returning the favor and visiting Janine and him.

Chapter 15
ONLY TWO LEFT IN THE NEST (AND ONE READY TO FLY)

Time was just going too fast. As Tom had skipped a grade, he was going to graduate before his eighteenth birthday. I felt he was much too young to move out of the house. I wanted to be sure that he had had the best opportunity possible to get to walk with the Lord and get a personal relationship with him. He seemed to show his grief and act out his sorrow at having lost his dad in different ways than the other two boys.

One day, I found him pounding his head against the wall in his bedroom and sobbing. When I went in, he said, "Why did God have to take my daddy?" Up until this time, he had said he planned to be a preacher like his dad. Now he changed his mind and decided he would be a scientist. He was good at that also, and I didn't argue with him. (I thought he would make an excellent lawyer because of his great ability to argue, but he didn't go for that.)

He and God would have to work that out, and they did. I'll tell more about that in the next chapter.

Tom was not afraid of work and held several jobs during high school. He had a paper route, in spite of scary dogs and people not paying their bills. He painted houses, even cleaned and painted a big building at the college in Eugene. That kind of worried me. He tried to plant trees on the side of the mountain, but that didn't work out. He then got on the Oregon Litter Patrol, picking up trash on the highway. His two favorite jobs were camp counselor and youth sponsor at the church. The kids really liked him, as he was so fun. He even ate ants to impress them. Ugh!

Track was Tom's sport, and he had a way of running his sport. We all knew he didn't have a kick at the end. He just ran full speed, steady all the time. As he came close to the finish line and others were passing him, I became hoarse yelling for him to "Kick it into gear, *now!*" I might as well have saved my breath. It wasn't long after Big Brother had begun running marathons that Tom wanted to run one too. Tom was made for marathons with his long, steady pace. He was very good at his preparation for the race and ran several miles each day. Marathons became a part of our family activities (and still are to this day).

As soon as Mike was old enough, his big brothers allowed him to join them in racing in a marathon. He had to be sixteen so the jarring of that long a run would not affect his bones adversely. I remember the first marathon they allowed him to run. They didn't expect him to get very far before a pick-up car would pick him up and bring him to the finish area. I stood on the sidelines and cheered them on. The two older boys finished, but where was Mike? No pick-up car had picked him up, and I hadn't seen him go by me. In spite of being completely exhausted, his brothers started backwards on the route to find their little brother. To the surprise of everyone (including Mike), he finished the race. He was hooked, but his brothers made him promise that next time, he would do his preparation running.

Tom got a spurt of growth after he left home, but his hormones were working well enough in high school that he could appreciate the female gender that God had created. He took a fancy to a little, cute Baptist girl in the grade below him. He got acquainted with her brother and thus got to see her a lot too. She did not show signs of being overly enthused about him, as she hoped to be a single medical missionary. She certainly was bright enough, but God had other plans.

Tom wanted to go on an amateur naturalist trip with the school. This kind of surprised me, and I wondered why he wanted to go. I soon found out why. After the trip, a picture emerged of him and Janine on the bus. She was sleeping, and he had his arm around her. They blew it up and put it up at school. Tom liked it; in fact, he still has the picture some thirty years later.

He was sad when Janine went off to California to college. He told me, "Mom, If God doesn't have Janine in mind for my life partner, but someone better, wow, I can hardly wait to see who she is! She must be something!"

And she was and is. God didn't get anyone new, just changed the mind of the girl with whom Tom had fallen in love. God did it through a dream. When she informed Tom of her change of mind, he promptly drove down to California on cloud nine, picked up the girl of his dreams, Janine, and drove her back to Springfield, where they later were married. I got to make and decorate their wedding cake. It turned out lovely.

They were married on my birthday. The wedding proved to be my undoing. As I walked down the aisle with Michael, I began to feel a draft on my back. My beautiful dress was zipped all the way to the neck, so no draft should be felt, but I definitely felt one. My zipper was a new kind (they don't use them anymore, and for good reason). It had unzipped from the bottom to the top, allowing my pantyhose, underpants, and bra to show. When I sat down, I tried to sooootch down in my seat, but a folding chair shows no mercy. Our doctor was sitting behind me and leaned forward to inform me of what I already was painfully aware of. When the ceremony was over, Mike stepped behind me to shield me on the way back down the aisle. When I got to the back, Hazel quickly zipped me down and back up, and all was well. As I stood in the reception line, everyone, it seemed, wanted to let me know what had happened to my gown. I simply smiled and told everyone, “It is fixed now.”

I did not get to make a spectacle of myself at Michael’s wedding, as he was married three thousand miles away and I could not afford the price of the plane ticket to get there and the motel expense. I did so want to go and knew that if his daddy had been alive, we would have gotten there. As Tom performed the wedding, I knew I missed something very special. But I am getting ahead of myself.

Chapter 16

"LORD, I ONLY HAVE ONE LEFT"

With Tom off to college and living on his own, that just left Mike and me. Actually, Tom was renting a house with a couple other Christian boys. As each boy left, it was a struggle for me to let them go and give them up for the Lord to finish raising them. Tom went to the University of Oregon and Northwest Christian College, which were in the town right next to us. I could still play mother and take him cookies and casseroles. His departure made it very hard on Mike, who was left, because Mike became my tennis partner, took golf lessons with me, and had to take vacations with me too. After our golf lessons, we would go out and play quite a lot at the nine-hole golf courses. Mike was so strong that he could get the ball on the green in one swing. It took me usually three, but I could drop it in the hole in one stroke. Mike had more trouble getting it in after he got it onto the green. We usually came out with about the same score. That was nice.

He was a good companion, and I appreciated him a lot. I dreaded the day when he would leave, but it would come all too quickly; but first, he had many a move to make with his mother as she tried to better herself in her profession as an optician.

Mike never had trouble getting a job, no matter where he was. When we were in Springfield, he took over his brother's paper route. When he got older, he worked at restaurants. He washed dishes and scrubbed potatoes at Western Sizzler. I enjoyed going there to eat too. Sometimes, he would have to spend the night cleaning and polishing the floors. They would be locked in, so I didn't worry too much.

When we lived in Salem, he got himself a job at a fish and chip house. He learned a lot and seemed to really enjoy it. It was nice that he could earn his own money.

When I went to Europe with Mom and Dad, he stayed with his big brother in Portland and worked at a fast food place. What I didn't know until later was that they got robbed a lot. I would have really been worried about him if I had known that.

I read about a Christian singles conference being held in LA at the Crystal Cathedral. The speakers and topics sounded wonderful, so I asked for the time off and bought my plane tickets. This time, my motel was very near the cathedral, and I had no problem walking. As it turned out, I would never be walking alone, anyway. The first day at registration, I smiled at a very good-looking man from the Middle East. In fact, he was heart-stoppingly handsome. He came over and introduced himself. After discussing our goals for the conference, we ended up signing up for the same classes. In fact, except for between ten PM and six AM, he was never more than two feet from me.

It turned out he was quite the poet, and he sent poems to me during class expressing his feelings toward me. I was soaking up all the attention and thoroughly enjoyed his company. It was fun learning about his life. He was an importer of cars and had a house in Chicago, one in LA, and one in Florida. His wife had died in a car wreck a year and a half ago. He had one son in college about the age of my Tim. He wanted me to come visit him.

"You may bring your mother with you if you wish. I have big houses and lots of bedrooms."

"That is certainly considerate of you to think of that, Sam."

It became apparent that this gentleman wanted for nothing, yet was very kind. As he had a dry sense of humor (which is what one of my grandparents had), I loved it. We were having a great time together.

The speakers were all inspirational and informative. Our classes were very helpful, and I took loads of notes. I think all

Sam did was write me poems, which did distract me somewhat when I read them and blushed.

As we sat in church the last day I discovered he had a beautiful, rich bass voice. It was fun singing the hymns with him. I was going to hate to say good-bye to him, but the time was fast approaching. I was glad his plane left before mine so I had some time alone to browse the bookstore and the educational materials.

I've been single now long enough that a constant companion hems me in, and I feel I need some space to breathe, I thought to myself. *Maybe I'll just be single the rest of my life. The Lord and I have lots of fun too.* The fact that flowers were waiting for me the next day after I got home and poems and letters kept coming in the mail did not change my mind.

I tried to kindly tell Sam I was no longer interested in continuing our relationship, but he would not accept that. I did not answer his letters and was always busy when he called, but he would not give up. What was I to do? My next move took care of the situation for me.

Chapter 17
JOBS AND THE SINGLE WOMAN

"This sure sounds interesting, Mike, but it's in Portland" (some one hundred miles away). "I think I'll check into it. Would you go with me for the interview?" I shouted over the TV one evening while reading the want ads in the paper.

" Sure, Mom."

"Tell me when you might be free, please, honey."

Thus it was that on a snowy Friday night after work, Mike and I headed up to Portland. We slipped and slid to a motel and spent the evening looking out the window watching the cars slipping and sliding on the highway just above us.

When we woke the next day and started out for breakfast, the snow was pretty deep, which made for a mess on the roadways. The curb and I kept wanting to bump into each other, but Mike would hop out and push the car back out again. Good thing I believe in starting early, as it took us a long time to get to my interview.

The interview seemed to go well. I had a three-ring notebook of all my certificates and accomplishments and accreditations. The owner had an opening in Mall 205, and that sounded like a fun place to work. *I could walk the mall on my lunch hours,* I thought,

Mike and I slid back home and then just had to wait for *the call.*

I had never applied for a job that I had not gotten, and I wondered if this might be the first.

"Mom, you better get that. It might be for you about the job." That was Mike's way of telling me he wasn't going to answer the phone.

"Monday? Yes, I suppose I could by then."

"You got the job, didn't you?" Mike excitedly responded to my look and smile.

"It will mean you will have to change high schools, you know." I wondered if he had thought about that.

He had, and responded, "I'd like to go to Aloha High School, as their sports are extra-good."

Not a problem, I thought. *I will go look at apartments in Aloha school district and just commute to work.* I drove up by myself the next day. It was not hard to find an apartment that suited me just fine. I put money down on it. I had brought some little kitchen things up with me but forgot there wouldn't even be a table to set them on. I had brought up a folding chair and piled everything on it and left happily for my soon-to-be-former home site.

As Monday was just a day away, it was too soon to move, so I would just commute until I could round up some friends and kids to help us move. After church, Mike and I started putting things in boxes until I piled wearily into bed at midnight.

What a way to start my first day on the new job, with too little sleep, I thought as I dozed off to sleep.

The next day, I drove up I-5 with all the trucks ever made. (Well, maybe there were a few missing, but not many.) "At least I don't have snow to contend with," I muttered.

I prayed a prayer of thanks and then began to sing. The hour-and-a-half drive went by quickly. My heart raced as I pulled into the mall and found a parking place.

I entered the optical store, where I saw a very big man with a big grin on his face looking me up and down.

"This is creepy," I told the Lord. *This surely is not the doctor,* I thought.

"Sure glad you are here with me, Lord."

I tried to ignore his rude behavior and walked over to introduce myself.

"Well, you might as well learn early. Go get me some coffee." His voice was gruff and not pleasant. Not a *please* in sight either.

"Okay." I smiled as sweetly as I could through clenched teeth. "Where is your cup?"

"In my office back there." He pointed to the back of

the store. I started to go back there, and he followed, but just before I was to pass through the small doorway to his room, he passed me and stood in the doorway sideways and motioned for me to pass through. I tried to ignore his obvious intention.

"I'm sorry, but with you standing in the doorway, there isn't enough room for me to pass through," I sweetly said, looking him straight in the eye.

"Well, you can try," he sneered.

Was this going to be a standoff? I hadn't even been there five minutes.

"Lord, what am I going to do?" I prayed.

Just then, a customer came in. "Thank you, Lord," I breathed. I helped the customer select frames and was sitting down to take measurements when a shadow fell across the desk. There "he" was.

"Joanne, I don't allow my opticians to take any measurements." Before I knew what was happening, he had pushed me off the stool and sat himself down.

I picked up my dignity (and the rest of me), walked to the telephone, and dialed the man who had hired me. When he picked up the phone and found out it was me, his first words were, "Don't quit, please. Come down and talk to me."

I agreed, grabbed my coat, and headed for the car. I called my eldest son, Tim, and told him I had just quit.

"Mom, you can't do that. You have two sons in college and one in high school. You can't not have a job. Don't quit."

When I told him why I had quit, he changed his tune and said, "Do you want me to come down and smash his face in?"

That made me laugh, and I felt better as I walked to my car to drive downtown to see the head boss man. My face was still red when he motioned me to sit down.

"Joanne, I know. You don't even have to tell me. I am so sorry. I thought he wouldn't do that to you. But I have an even better job for you, but it is in Salem. I will give you a percentage of the profit plus many bonuses. You will be in charge of the eyewear section, and the doctor you'll be working with is a perfect gentleman." (He turned out to be just that.)

I accepted his very generous offer, drove to Aloha and got my money back on the apartment I had rented (but had not moved a thing into yet, except a folding chair), and headed for my home in Springfield. I was still fuming as I crawled wearily into bed. I was so glad Michael was willing to eat cold cereal for supper at night when I was too tired to cook. He could down a mixing bowl full of the stuff and never complain.

To commute from Salem was not nearly as bad as from Portland. The next weekend, Mike and I drove up to Salem to house hunt. We found a very cute, but small, house for rent on the south side of town. As I was raised in a very small house, I did not need a lot of space. Michael had lived in all sizes of houses and could adapt well. The price was right and, we took it.

"Please don't chip the glass on the coffee table," I implored them, but it was too late.

"Are you sure that old record player that belonged to your grandparent Kings won't fall out of the truck?" (It did fall out and split in a thousand pieces.) They say moving three times is the same as having a fire. I believe it.

"Just things, Mama, just things," the boys tried to comfort me. No, it was just memories.

It took the boys, plus help from some friends and their husbands, to transfer everything we owned to the new location. Our new home was about an hour away from our Springfield home.

The boys helped me put the pictures on the walls.

"Mom, it's time you tried to move on now. Don't put Dad's picture up this time."

I couldn't believe what Tim was saying. Of course I'd put John's picture up, right along with all the rest of the family. When all five pictures were up in a row in the hall, I sat down to rest. *Jiggle, jiggle, jiggle.*

"What was that strange noise?" I wondered out loud, with a little apprehension! It came from the hall, so I cautiously crept in there. To my shock, John's picture was rattling. I hunted for a furnace vent, thinking the wind from something was blowing it. I found nothing. So I just moved his picture to the other end of the line of pictures where mine was and traded places with him.

I had just sat down to read again when I heard it again. Thinking it was just some breeze from somewhere rattling my picture, I went again into the hall. To my amazement, it was again John's picture rattling. *Why, how could this be?*

So I put his picture in the center of all our pictures and marched to the kitchen to start supper.

Then I heard a *rattle, rattle, crash.* I ran into the hall, and John's picture was on the floor. The glass in the picture had broken too this time.

"Okay, Lord, I think I get the hint."

So with tears in my eyes, I sadly put his picture in my top drawer.

It was Sunday, at last, and Mike and I headed for our new church. There were lots of young people, and Mike got acquainted right away. It seems a lot of them went to a private Christian school across the river, and of course, Mike wanted to go there too. I thought this was a good idea, as I thought it would be easier for him to walk with the Lord at a Christian school. I found it still took some doing. I had to drive him to school, which was a ways up the river on a hill. Not a fun drive when there was snow. The next year, he transferred to the public school and did just fine.

My work at the new optical shop went very well. I really enjoyed it and the wonderful doctor I worked with. I got bonuses for every person I signed up for an eye exam, for adding tints, and for any extras that they wanted. My paycheck doubled. I was really socking it away, as Mike and I didn't spend much and the bank was just a few steps away from my work.

My former boss in Eugene had his motorcycle for sale and offered it to us for a very reasonable price. Mike thought he would like it. He did need transportation for his job and school, so we bought it. Things were going well until I received a notice that I had to appear in court because Michael had gotten a ticket for speeding.

On the appointed day, I took off work, and off we went to the courthouse. When it was our turn, a lady policewoman, who had given him the ticket, took the stand. She told me I should be grateful she stopped him, as he was traveling on a back gravel road very fast.

"If he had to stop, he would not have been able to, but just would have slid and no doubt would have crashed. He could have easily been killed," she concluded.

On the way home, I informed him we would be taking the cycle back to Eugene and seeing if we could get our money back. I did not get too much objection. He paid his own ticket out of his work money. We had lived through another crisis.

"Mom, Tom's on the line, and it sounds urgent."

It must be, I thought, as it was late at night and I was ready for bed.

"Yes. Of course, I'll be right down."

I dressed and headed out the door.

"I'll be back as soon as I can. Your brother has something to tell me that can't wait."

His girlfriend was still in California, so I knew it probably didn't have anything to do with that relationship.

"Lord, help me to say the right thing," I prayed as I drove the hour drive in the pouring rain. Rain did not bother me, as that is just part of living in the wonderful state of Oregon. It was the first time I had gone to his new apartment, and I was having a hard time finding it. It was hidden behind another building. I ran to the door and knocked. It was so good to get a nice hug from my son.

"Mom, you know I have been fighting the Lord, as I didn't want to be a minister after Dad died. Well, tonight, while doing a science project in the basement of the university, I told the Lord, 'I give up. I will do whatever you want me to do.' So, Mom, tomorrow I will register at Northwest Christian College, where you and Dad went."

We both cried. I knew his daddy would be so happy and proud.

All the way back to Salem, I sang and cried.

Mike and I had not lived in Salem over a year when the nice optometrist that I worked with bought out another optical shop in downtown Salem and was leaving. My boss called me in and offered me a job in Eugene.

Salem had been good to Mike and me. He got to be the chairperson for the International Relations Week (which is a model United Nations). He was considering going into politics as a career. He would have been very good. With his speaking ability, good looks, and personality, he would have been a shoo-in.

Springfield would also be good to us. Mike was in a quartet that went to state competition. He played a singing role in *Fiddler on the Roof* and one in *The Music Man,* all the while holding down a job in a local restaurant and competing in track. You'd think all this would keep him out of trouble, but *no.* I am just now finding out things he did that make me fall to my knees in gratitude that God took care of him. He could have easily been killed or crippled diving off the Hayden Bridge, or dashing across a four-lane freeway to get home via a "shortcut," or driving my new car where he could do wheelies. Wrecked the car, but he lived.

I was happy with the rental house that I found in Springfield. It was a straight shot to my work at the mall and not too far from Mike's high school. Once again, I had fun decorating. The landlord even humored me and put in a corner stove. It was the next best thing to a fireplace. The kitchen, though small, put out some mighty good meals for a lot of people. I even decorated two seven-layer wedding cakes in it and one anniversary cake that was transported, in parts, over five hundred miles to its destination.

My work was fun. I was learning a lot and having fun doing it. Some of my patients didn't, however.

"Joanne, this man wants contacts. Would you instruct him, please?" my nice optometrist asked.

"Come on in and have a seat," I instructed the huge logger. I noticed his hands were very rough and very large. This was not going to be easy. It proved to be far worse than I imagined. Every time he brought his finger, with the contact on it, up close to his eye, he would back away. Then, without warning, he slumped to the floor in a dead faint. Now, to get him up would be no easy task, as my area was like a long, narrow closet with a long shelf that he was facing. When he came to, he was embarrassed, and we called off the session for the day and went out to choose some nice glasses. He came back in a few days and did well enough to take the contacts home. His vision was probably better in the contacts, but my guess is that he wore his glasses more often.

While I was having lunch one day, my former boss called me and offered me a job. I was now getting health insurance and I knew they didn't have any for their employees. He said they would get some and I would get a good salary. I really enjoyed the people who worked at my old job so did decide to change jobs. It proved to be a good move for me.

Chapter 18
SECOND VACATION AS A SINGLE (OH MY!)

My sister's husband was a chaplain in the air force, stationed in Germany. It was the year of the passion play that they put on every ten years. My folks were going and invited me to go along. They said they would pay my way and all I would need to do was have money for anything special that I wanted, like souvenirs. This seemed too good to be true. It turned out it was. Mike went to Portland to stay with his big brother and work at a fast food restaurant while I was gone.

I knew the plane trip (about which, remember, I don't like to fly) was going to be long. I tried to settle back and relax, but a turbaned, bearded man behind me let out a scream that sent chills up and down my spine and stood my hair on end (well, not really on end, but you get the picture). He took the back of my seat and shook it. The stewardess came and tried to talk to him, but he became more violent. She turned to me and said, "He doesn't understand English" My guess is he did. By the time we taxied into the London airport, my nerves were shot, as he had continued screaming and shaking my chair all the way over. We had a layover in London, and I tried to get a little sleep in the airport, but to no avail. I was so glad when we finally arrived in Germany and my sister and her husband were there to help us with our luggage. My sister's husband's nephew, Neil, came with us too. The trip was his graduation present. However, when we arrived in Germany, his luggage was either taken by someone else or traveled to another destination. That was not a fun experience for him. My sister borrowed some clothes from her neighbor, who had a boy about Neil's size. The luggage was later sent over to the base, and he was able to have his own things once again.

My sister and her husband were stationed at Hahn Air Force Base in Germany, so we toured out from there. *Volks walks* are very popular there, and we decided to participate in the John Wayne Volks Walk.

As we were going through the forests, we kept seeing these signs that said "Beware of Wolf," "Lobo." I kept my eye peeled but never did encounter one. That was okay by me. We all received John Wayne medals for the walk—my first and last "Volks" walk.

One evening, after an exhausting day, Neil and I decided to take a little walk. It didn't take long to settle into the lodging for the night, as my room was up a flight of stairs, then through a closet door and there was a mattress on the floor. I dropped my suitcase on the floor by the mattress, and we were off.

After walking for a while, we saw a tent out in a field and decided to go investigate. The closer we got, the more curious we became. We couldn't figure out what it was. So we lifted the flap and popped in. It was a circus. Now, as neither of us had brought any money, we just quickly found an empty seat and sat down.

"I hope we don't get thrown in jail for sneaking into the circus and not paying," I whispered to Neil. What a fun time we had, and we were able to sneak out before it was over without getting caught. We ran back to our lodging, as it was getting late. I was so glad Neil had come on the trip too. He and I were able to do a lot of fun things together throughout the trip.

It was such fun seeing all the castles and hearing the stories that go with them. Then the time came to go to Oberammergau to see the passion play. We were lodged in the home of the actors. They fed and bedded us but took the faucets off the tub spigots, as we didn't pay to take a bath. (We bathed at the famous indoor/outdoor pool and Jacuzzi nearby.

The play went on all day but took a break for lunch. The poor actors had to come home and prepare lunch for us, then scurry back to the play. Besides our group at the home, there were some Canadians there also. They were fun to get to know. The man of the house and his son were woodcarvers. Everyone bought something. The woman of the house did ceramics. You guessed it—everyone bought something. I'm sure the year the play was on helped the family budget a lot.

I don't know if it was a misunderstanding, or if Mom and Dad changed their minds, or what, but every time we ate out, I was having to pay for my own. My money was running very low by the time we got to the play. I didn't know what to do. I was sitting on my bed crying and praying and had just decided I would need to end my trip and fly home right away. Flying all by myself was not a popular idea with me. Mother came in and asked me what was wrong, and I explained. She said they would do as they had said so I wouldn't have to go home alone. The play was worth all the fuss and muss. The trip was a wonderful adventure, but I have no desire to go back. When I got home, I found all had gone well on the home front.

Chapter 19
MEN DO STRANGE THINGS

After I got back, I was told about a singles group at one of our churches in downtown Eugene. I was glad they told me because the chairman of the board where John and I had served in Springfield called me over to his house one evening. He very kindly informed me that the preacher would prefer that I not continue to go to that church anymore. He felt that my presence detracted from his ministry, as too many people felt loyal to John. Thus, I started going to the singles group downtown.

Now, there were some interesting single men there, and one began coming out to visit and play board games and cards with my parents and me. He was very nice, and the relationship was going nicely, I thought. Then one Wednesday night, he kissed me goodnight, invited me to a movie Friday night, and left, never to be seen again. Friday night came and went, but he did not show up. At church Sunday, I asked about him and was told he had flown to Las Vegas Thursday and gotten married.

Another fellow from the group invited me to a concert. It was very nice. The evening was nice. Before he left, he said, "I'll see you Sunday." He walked out of my house, drove over to another lady's house, and asked her to marry him. He was engaged when I said "Hi" to him at church the next Sunday.

I am having a strange effect on men, I mused. My best friend, Hazel, asked me to come with her to their Model T club banquet. There was a fellow that needed a date. I told her that I had gone on so many blind dates that I should qualify for a dog. But, yes, I would go. I was hoping my blind date would not *be* a dog. He wasn't! Riding in his old Model T was lots of fun, and the banquet was lovely. Then a lady came in, alone and late. She plopped herself down next to me and just glared at me. I turned and introduced myself with a smile. But she pulled herself up straight and said very huffily, "I know who you are. You have my boyfriend. I want him back."

"Well," I whispered to my friend Hazel, "this is going to be a lovely evening."

When it was time for us to go home, she grabbed what she perceived to be "her man" and pulled him outside. I asked Hazel if I couldn't please just ride home with her. I did. I did not date him anymore.

I was ready to just bow out of the dating scene and concentrate on other things, but a man named Ralph was in a Christian singles group a friend and I started attending after church on Sundays. He was good-looking, drove a sports car, and seemed to have plenty of money. After a few dates, I knew we would never be anything but "just friends," as there just wasn't any "spark" there. I wanted a "spark" or forget it. Mike would soon be gone, and then I would be all alone. The Lord and I could handle it, I knew!

Chapter 20
NOW I WAS REALLY ALONE!

As Mike was about to go into the air force, I thought it best to move to a smaller place and buy it for an investment, rather than continue renting. I wanted someplace that was safe. Not far from where I worked stood a tall condominium building that looked appealing. The price seemed within my range, and the view was great from my fifth-floor living room.

"I'll take it," I heard myself saying, even though my knees were shaking. Again, family and friends moved all my furniture and "stuff." This time, nothing was broken. Isn't that remarkable? Mike was there only a few short months, and then he was off to the service.

He called it "the old folks' home." It served me well. I felt safe, but I shouldn't have!

One day, as I was down in the basement doing my laundry, a man came in. He was big and burly. You know, the type that could go bear hunting with a switch. To my utter surprise, he took off his shirt and then his undershirt. I was getting a creepy feeling. He gradually walked in front of me so he was blocking the one and only door. This was scary, and I didn't know what I should do.

Then he proceeded to take off his shoes and socks. I knew I didn't want to make eye contact with him, nor did I want to talk to him. Next, off came his trousers. Now I was getting scared!

"Lord, help me think what I should do. He is much too big for me to defend myself."

He was pulling down his undershorts, and I reasoned that his feet would be held in place just before he stepped out of his shorts, so he wouldn't be able to run after me. I would just have to run past him and try to avoid any swinging arms that might come my way. That's just what I did. So, after taking a deep breath, I made my feet run, and did manage to get by him just as he was bending down.

Not bothering to take the elevator, I dashed up the one flight of stairs to the office and breathlessly told them what was happening down in the laundry room. They called the police, and the naked man was taken away. After retrieving my clothes from the dryer and reaching my apartment safely, I sank into my big chair. I was so glad I had a bolt on my door. I tried to compose myself. I wonder if he was ever able to get his clothes out of the washer.

Just then, the phone rang. My nerves were on edge, so I really jumped.

"We're going to the fair tonight, and our friend from your building wants to go with us and would like to take you. Would you go?" This was a couple from the church that I liked very much.

What if it is the same man I just had an encounter with? I thought. Chances were pretty slim of that, so I said, "Sure, it would be fun."

I was pleasantly surprised when the tall, nice-looking, smiling man showed up at my door with my friends. We walked to the fair, and he held my hand. We had a really great time. He was certainly well-known, as everyone, it seemed, wanted him to stop and talk with them.

When they brought me home, I invited everyone in, and we had hot chocolate and cinnamon rolls and visited until late. When he left, I thought, *Now, he'll be fun to do things with, as we had had such a fun evening together.*

The next evening, I was not surprised when the phone rang and it was him.

"I'm going to make some biscuits but need to borrow some baking powder."

"Sure, I'll bring it right up."

I grabbed a couple of cinnamon rolls too. He was three floors higher than I was, so I decided to take the elevator, not the stairs. I didn't want to arrive all out of breath. As I approached his apartment, I heard female laughter. I turned to walk away, but the door had opened, and a woman, scantily dressed, said, "Yes?"

"Oops! I guess I have the wrong apartment."

But before I could escape, Ralph appeared and reached for the rolls, saying, "I'll call you later."

What was that all about? I wondered. When I was back in my apartment and my face had stopped being red, I could imagine them both eating my cinnamon rolls.

The next day, he called me and thanked me and said it was his sister.

"Yeah, right!" If it had been his sister, he would have introduced me and invited me in. *I must look awfully dumb and gullible,* I thought. I never dated him again.

Some days later, I decided I would help the Lord out (do my part, you know) in getting me a date. So when I developed a bad toothache, I made an appointment with a Christian dentist that was a widower. I had been told how nice he was. When the time came, I took my book on widows, and headed for his office. It wasn't far, so I just walked. I thought he would just take an X-ray and actually do any work on any teeth at a later time.

When my name was called, I scurried in and sat in his chair with the book on my lap and the title *Widows* in plain view. He was very good-looking and very nice. To my surprise, he looked at my teeth, gave me a shot, and proceeded to pull one of my back teeth. This accomplished two things. I was very embarrassed, and my face began to swell and hurt. By the time I made it back to work, I was a mess. I sat in the boss's office, but it only got worse.

"You'd better just go on home, Joanne. You look awful," he informed me.

"I'm so sorry!" I told the boss. "I thought he wouldn't do anything on the first visit."

Things had not turned out as I had planned at all.

Another time things did not turn out as I had planned came about a month later. I had been appointed as chairman of the state optical convention, and we had a planning meeting coming up in Portland, just an hour and a half away. One of my church friends knew an elder in a rural church that had a plane.

"He'd be glad to fly you up to your meeting, I'm sure," she told me one evening. "He's single, too," she added for incentive.

Thus, one beautiful, star-filled evening, I hurried from work to the airport and climbed aboard Keith's small plane. Now, somehow, I enjoy small planes but not big ones. I feel like I could escape the small ones easier if they should crash, I guess.

The ride up to Portland was wonderful. Keith was an excellent pilot. It was hard to talk with the engine noise, but we did manage. I was having a very nice time. He landed smoothly, but then, I discovered, the hard part came. I had not had time to change my shoes so still had on my high heels. In his small plane, one must dismount off the wing. As I started to step down, my heel got caught in the wing flap, and I fell (not gracefully) to the cement below. I landed on my knees, tore my nylons, and began to bleed all over me and the ground. The pain was awful. He helped me up, and I hobbled into the airport office and cleaned up somewhat. All through the meeting, the pain was getting worse and worse. The restaurant was able to get me some Band-Aids and an aspirin. This helped a lot.

Somehow, I made it through the meeting, and we headed home. Except for the pain, the ride home was beautiful. What I would remember was twinkling stars, a good companion that made me laugh, and a good feeling about the meeting. We had done a nice job of planning. I had an exceptionally good committee to work with.

The next day, I went to my doctor, and he took X-rays. They showed that I had chipped my knees. He said, "You will have arthritis in those knees someday too." How right he was!

When I got home, I called my pilot friend to see if he had insurance that might cover the doctor, but when a woman answered, I hung up. We only had one date after that, and then he got himself engaged to that other woman.

"Would you mind dropping off these frames to Jim's Optical after work tonight, Joanne?" my boss asked while handing me a package.

"Why, sure," I replied. *No big deal,* I thought. Was I ever wrong!

It was dark by the time I got off work, and I hurriedly walked toward my condominium with the package under my arm.

Now, to get to Jim's, I had to cross a huge empty lot the size of a city block. I started across and was aware that it was extra-dark. One of the streetlights had burnt out. Out of the corner of my eye, I caught the image of a disheveled, dirty, unshaven, burly man. I wondered if this was the same man I had encountered in the laundry room. He was walking toward me on the sidewalk. I decided to cut across that empty lot. About halfway across the empty lot, I heard footsteps behind me coming quite fast. I sped up my pace. He sped up his pace. They footsteps still got closer.

Oh my, should I run for the door of the building? That would look foolish, but I don't want to become a statistic, I thought. As the footsteps got closer, I decided to make a run for it. After all, there was a whole empty city block; why would someone be right behind me? Having worked out at the gym for years, I figured I could beat him. I could hear him breathing right by my shoulder by the time I reached for the door and swung myself in. I ran to the reception desk and turned around just in time to see the man turn from the door and *walk* on past, looking in the windows. My heart was racing so fast. After I delivered my package and rested, it was time to start back.

"We'll watch from the door until you get across the vacant lot," Jim encouraged me. I was so glad my condominium had a bolt on the door. I loved walking to work and hated the thought that for safety's sake, I might have to drive my car.

Chapter 21
A NEW JOB

One day, the owner of an optical frame company came into the optical shop to see me. He needed a sales rep and wondered if I would like to work for him. I had no obligations at home now, so thought it might be fun. It would turn out to be very adventurous.

I bought a series of tapes that I could play in the car. They were all on how to sell. My job was to go cold turkey to a mall, find the optical shops, present myself, and then interest the buyers in viewing my frames. Lugging the suitcases, full of frames, was not easy, especially while wearing high heels, but I learned to manage.

Some of the other reps from different companies helped me pick safe, clean, cheap motels. If any of the other reps were in an area at the same time as I was, they would invite me to go out with them for supper. I learned a lot from them.

Often, while swimming in the motel pool, I would get acquainted with other salesmen, from book reps to you-name-it reps. Many times, they would invite me to eat with them in the motel dining room. This I would do, but I always paid my own way. That way, I would feel no obligation to them. I could just enjoy their company. And enjoy their company I did. Salesmen are always good conversationalists, so the evening would just slip by. Usually, we would both have seven-thiry AM or eight AM appointments, so it was no problem to say good night early. I never stayed up late.

One nice benefit of being a sales rep was the fact that you needed a good car. I bought me a Delta 88 and really liked it. I soon discovered that it had a problem: the belts kept slipping off, or snapping off, at very inopportune times. I was coming down a mountain in eastern Washington and had just rounded a corner when I heard this horrible sound. I knew I had to stop, but couldn't pull over, as I was on the cliff side of the highway and there simply wasn't any space. I coasted further down the mountain, found a place, and was able to stop. What now? Cell phones weren't invented yet. I hopped out and flagged down the next vehicle, which happened to be a truck. He took me to the nearest town (which wasn't very near).

Everything was closed.

"Okay, Lord, what do I do now?"

I found a motel, checked in, and spent the night. The next

day, I called a service station. He just happened to have the belt I needed, and we were off to the car. He was able to fix it, but told me the motor had been mounted crookedly and the belts would continue to break.

"You'd better take it in and have them fix it correctly. This might be a recall item. You could really get yourself in a lot of trouble." I followed his advice. It was a recall, and they fixed it.

About that time, I was having some other problems. My sales business was just doing great. I figured I should have been making some good money. Then my paycheck came, along with a readout of my sales. Many of my sales were not on there. What could be the problem? I drove up to the main office and asked for a readout of my sales. When it came shooting out of the machine, I looked at it, and nothing was amiss. Then why were many of my sales not on my paycheck slip? When I asked about it, they said, "Oh, the boss takes those for company sales, and you don't get paid for them."

I was *furious!*

"My boss is a post turtle!" I hissed. "At least, that's what Texans call people like him. You know a post turtle is one that didn't get there by himself. He doesn't belong there, and he can't get anything done while he's up there." All those in the office laughingly agreed.

The boss was there, so I marched into his office and suggested he pay me what he owed me and not do that again.

Which he reluctantly did, kind of. Paid some, but not quite all he owed. Then I quit.

I knew Proverbs 23:10 said not to *defraud* the widow. Luke 20:47 says God's heaviest sentence awaits those who cheat widows. In fact, I knew of twenty-seven scriptures about promises to widows and how they should be treated. I decided to just let God take care of it. Within a year, the man was out of business and had lost his wife through divorce.

My dear, sweet daddy wanted to sue him, but I knew I could not handle going in and out of court, so just took the extra money he gave me and considered it a big lesson. The other sales reps knew exactly what I was talking about. I had made a lot of money and had had a lot of fun too.

For instance, there was that time in Seattle when I was swimming in the hotel pool and an old schoolmate came by and said, "Joanne, get dressed, and I'll take you to dinner."

Which I promptly did. He took me to the top of the Space Needle. What elegant dining it was. The view, of course, was spectacular! The food was yummy! After a laughter-filled, delicious meal, we decided to walk around in the park below. We stumbled upon a group who were playing all sorts of instruments in a big, empty warehouse. My date grabbed me, and we began to dance. We were the only ones there. What fun! That really drove my adrenaline level high. In junior high, he and I used to dance together at the YWCA. We would have such fun jitterbugging. He would pull me under his legs, and then I'd jump up. I wasn't sure I was up to all that now, but I was certainly willing to try. I always get caught up in the music. We left about an hour later, all sweaty and exhausted. What fun! Before he said goodnight, he asked me when I would be back.

"I will have a surprise for you then."

I could hardly wait.

Later that year, when I came back to Seattle, he had gotten tickets to *The King and I* at one of the playhouses in Seattle. He and I had been in several musical plays together in high school, so he knew I really enjoyed them. I was so excited to get to see Yul Brynner. Alas, when the curtain went up, we were told that Yul Brynner was ill and would not be taking his part. The one who did take it, his understudy, was really good, so I really didn't care.

That night, I stayed at the YWCA, which was not in a very good part of town. All night, I heard noises, talking, and yelling on the street below. In the night, I had to knock cockroaches off the toilet seat. As fast as I chased them off, more would come running around the seat. They scooted so fast. I hated to think about sitting down on their freeway. The sheets on my almost nonexistent mattress were dirty too. I felt this was a one-time experience at the YWCA in Seattle.

The next morning, as daylight crept in over the Seattle harbor, I snuck down the stairs and headed for my parked car, a block away. Again, I was in high heels, because I had an appointment that morning. It is hard to walk softly in high heels, but believe me, I tried. I noticed two men leaning up against my car and smoking. It made me wonder how safe it would be for me to try to put my suitcases in the trunk of the car. I always dragged my suitcases, full of frames, into wherever I slept. One sales rep left them in her car, and in the morning, they were gone. When the streetlight turned green, I knew I would have to at least try to ignore the men and somehow get my trunks in the car.

"Lord, You do know I am here, don't you?"

As if in answer, a policeman rounded the corner just ahead of me and arrived at my car the same time I did. The two men sauntered off. The policeman helped lift my suitcases into my trunk, and with a "thank you," I was off.

"Thank you, Father," I also muttered to my kind, and faithful, God.

Now, there was a downside to my selling job too. I was raised in the country, where the highway was very narrow. When you met a car, it was a close call. There was no yellow line to help you stay on your side of the road. Now I found myself in Seattle with twelve lanes. Lanes would merge and force you to exit whether you wanted to or not. Thus I found myself crossing over a small bay out to a peninsula where I didn't need to go.

My gas was getting low, so as soon as I could, I exited and found a service station. Now, in Washington, you pump your own gas. I took diesel, which stinks. As I am not really dainty when pumping gas, I got it all over me and really began to smell.

I didn't want to waste my time and gas, so I hunted up an optical shop, and in spite of my smelly new perfume, I dragged my suitcases in and was able to make a big sale.

Chapter 22
"NOW WHAT, LORD?"

After Michael left home, I knew it was time to consider what I should do with my life. I received a letter asking if I would be interested in applying for a job as director of an orphanage in Guatemala. That seemed like an excellent opportunity to serve again. I loved children and felt it would be right up my alley. I had not forgotten my Spanish language, so that would not be a problem. I filled out the application and sent it in. I didn't even bother to pray about it. It was a slam dunk, I thought. But when the reply came back with a contract, I decided I had better stop and talk to the Lord about this. To my great surprise, when I asked the Lord about it, the reply I felt he told me was a big *no. How could this be?* I thought. It seemed so perfect to me. So I knelt down by my bed and talked to Him again. Again, I felt I was getting a *no.* Sadly, I wrote my letter to them and declined the offer.

"Well, Lord, what *do* you have in mind for me?" I asked.

Tim was teaching up in Portland by a new mall that was just going in.

"Mom, why don't you come up and look it over for an optical shop of your own? I can help you get a doctor to come in with you. In fact, I think there is one looking to move there now. I could help you advertise by having my school kids pass out leaflets."

Well, it did sound interesting, and then I would be close to one of my kids. So the next weekend, I drove up to look it over. It looked good, and I was seriously considering it. Right across the highway was an apartment complex, so I thought I would check it out too.

It turned out to be a singles' apartment complex. Well, that was interesting!

While I was in the office talking about renting an apartment, one of the singles came up to me and said, "Don't worry about what your apartment looks like. You won't be in it much. We usually sleep with our boyfriends. It doesn't take long to find one."

I left. I didn't think this was the place for me.

The next weekend, Mom and Dad came down to look over the mall too. The trouble was that my support group was in Eugene. A widow definitely needs a support group. I thought it best to not move up to Portland now.

It was not very long before the Lord did show me what

he wanted for me. Dorothy, my friend from a Christian singles group, popped by the optical shop and dropped off an application.

"You'll have to fill it out on your break and run it by the chairman's house tonight, as today is the deadline."

During my next break, I did take the application to the break room to look it over. It was an application to be the house director of Chi Omega at the University of Oregon in Eugene. I would be "mom" to 129 girls. My boys thought I ought to apply for a fraternity instead, as I had raised boys.

"Lord, is this from you? You always wait until the last minute with me," I prayed as I filled out the application. I seemed to be getting a definite *"yes!"*

So off I drove, right after work, to find the address on the application. If it was to be, then I would not be too late. If it was not to be, then I would be too late. I was not worried either way.

That night, I received a phone call from the chairman of the Chi Omega staff.

"Will you please come have an interview with me tomorrow? We are very excited about your application."

The next day, I drove up to the beautiful home of the chairman and walked in to meet the nice lady that would determine the direction my life would be taking. The interview went well, and I walked away from that house the new director of the Chi Omega Sorority at the University of Oregon in Eugene.

"Lord," I pleaded, "I've never even belonged to a sorority. You are really going to have to help me here." And of course, He did!

I was aware that often the Lord's work is not for wimps, so that forces us to depend on Him. As we come out of fiery trials, we become strong as steel.

I was to live in the sorority house twenty-four/seven. That would save me rent and groceries. My new living space was very small, almost claustrophobic, but adequate. I was right on the alley next to a noisy frat house. They furnished me with a parking space for my car right next to my room. I discovered this was not always a good thing. My car was soon being used to climb up to the roof of my little apartment, and then over to the girls' bedrooms. I would hear screaming at all hours of the night, as the girls left their windows open and the boys took advantage of that. Many a night, I would have to put on my bathrobe, climb the stairs, and try to evict the frat boys. I was confident I could do it. The definition of confident in this case was "the feeling you have just before you understand the situation." Now, drunk, big football players with hormones raging at the sight of pretty girls in baby doll PJs are not always cooperative. The Eugene police and I got very well acquainted, as I often had to call them.

I soon found out why the Lord had put me in that spot. One after the other of the 129 girls would come knocking on my door and ask to come talk. I could not believe my ears at the tales they were telling me. My heart, and often my eyes, cried. There was no law against me sharing my faith with them and helping them to get rooted once again in their faith. We prayed together. They gave me great respect, and I loved them, and they felt it. I would have done anything for them and they for me. It was a good match.

Once again, I found myself depending on my sons for help. The generational clichés that the girls used were unknown to me. Some called them "valley girls." They would put "like" anywhere in the sentence. It would make no sense at all. They also used "ya know?" a thousand times in a day. But there were times expressions were totally foreign to me. I would call one of my boys and ask him, "What does this word mean?" I always got help when I needed it, which was often. Each generation has their own vocabulary, and as I was not around girls of that age a lot in my work, I really needed help. It was kind of fun, but I embarrassed myself sometimes by not always knowing what those words meant. Sometimes, I felt it was almost like a different language.

During spring break and Christmas break, I could leave the house. So I flew to Texas to see my middle son, Thomas, and his sweet wife Janine. I had such fun playing with my darling granddaughters. This was such a blessing. Whenever possible, I also scooted up to my eldest son, Tim's, in Portland to hold and play with my first grandson. Life was good, and I was happy. Only God knew the big change that was about to take place and that would forever change my life.

While having devotions one morning, I asked the Lord to

show me a sign that He was real, and not just my imagination. You may wonder how I could have doubts about God after all He had done for me. Well, it puzzles me too, but the Bible is full of people like me.

He seemed to be telling me to write down in my devotional book where I would like to go that would be impossible without His intervention. So I said to my dear heavenly Father, "Well, Lord, all my kids have been to Hawaii, but I haven't, so I'd like to go there. *But,* please, Lord, not with someone on a diet. I want to enjoy myself, and, oh yes, not my parents either. That would be too easy."

Now, I knew this was a pretty big order, but I put it in my devotional book and just forgot it. Later on that same year, the Lord would remind me of his promise.

A holiday was coming up, and I would have several days off. This would be a good time to go visit my junior high and high school girlfriend Carol, who had just discovered she had cancer. She only lived twelve hours away in California. My old junior high boyfriend, Robert, said he would pick me up and we'd go together. He and I had double-dated with Carol and her now-husband, Jim. Many a time we had gone dancing at the YWCA together. To go see them sounded like loads of fun to me, and it was. At a restaurant on the way down, we stopped and played Pac-Man on one of their machines. It was a really popular game. I could see why. I had never played this game before, but found it to be great fun. Poor Robert had to threaten to go on without me to get me to stop.

Robert and I were both in choir together in school, so had a lot of fun singing some of our old choir songs. It made the miles just speed away. It was a joyous long weekend. We made a lot of nice memories, but it was nice to get back to Chi Omega and to my lovely girls. I only saw my girlfriend Carol once more before she left this earth. She left a big hole in my heart.

There usually was a truck that pulled up in the alley early in the morning and delivered groceries to our chef. However, one day, the chef asked me to pick up a few things that he had forgotten at the grocery store. As I had not shopped for a long time, it was kind of fun. As I was putting my groceries into the trunk of my car, I noticed a lady in the car next to me holding the back of her head and looking very frightened. I knocked on her window, and she rolled down her window just a crack.

"Are you okay?"

"No," she whispered.

"How can I help you?"

"I have called the police," she said. "I have been shot in the back of the head, and my brains are oozing out."

I looked closer, and sure enough, under her hand, which was held to her head, there was something kind of white and doughy. So I looked closer and saw an empty, opened can of biscuits. It was lying at the top of her grocery bag, which was on the back seat of her car.

"I bet the expiration date on that can of biscuits was way overdue, and it had exploded with a bang, hitting her in the back of the head. She probably reached up and felt something and thought it was her brains coming out," I reasoned out loud.

Boy, will the 911 crew get a laugh out of this, I thought.

Just then, the 911 people pulled up, so I left. She had put her window up and clearly didn't want to talk to me anymore. *Who would believe this?* I wondered.

Chapter 23
I'M ADJUSTING TO SINGLE LIFE!

While reading the paper one day, I noticed that one of the churches nearby was having a well-known singles speaker. He would be speaking on a Tuesday night. I was free that night. *Why not go?* I thought. So I did.

As the speaker began to speak, he really seemed to connect with me and my thinking. I was taking notes as fast as I could. When I got home, I pulled out my notes and started to read.

"God is preparing you for His pick and preparing him for you. Maybe one of you is not ready yet."

That helped a lot. I just relaxed after that and stopped looking for a single man. I became a happy single. If God had anyone for me, He would just have to drop him in my lap, as I was through looking.

I was adjusting to the single life just fine, until our church had a session on "The Gifts of the Holy Spirit." At the end of the sessions, we all had to take a test. Then the pastor would call us and make an appointment to come talk to him about it.

"Joanne, would Monday at three o'clock be all right with you?" my pastor asked me.

"Sure, I'll be there."

On Monday at three o'clock, I prayerfully entered the pastor's office, not knowing what to expect. When we were seated, he got my test out and said "Joanne, you definitely do not have the gift of celibacy."

Well, I thought, *what am I supposed to do? Go pull someone off the street?*

But the pastor continued.

"You are going too fast. No one can run fast enough to catch up to you. Slow down. Also, you put your requirements higher than the Lord does. You say, 'No divorced man.' Well, some Christian men are divorced through no fault of their own. Just be more open to what the Lord may be sending you."

I left a little discouraged as I trudged back to my car, not knowing just what I was supposed to do.

That night, I received a phone call from an elder in our church, Dale. He wanted to know if I would like to go to the basketball game at the U of O. Dale was one who had helped me move many a time, and so I said, "Yes."

I did not consider it a date. I figured he just wanted to take me so he would have a parking place by the gym. I had been single eight years now, so I figured if he had wanted to date me, he would have done it before now.

When he came, I was ready, and off we went. We yelled and had a really good time. He held my hand on the way home, and I felt "sparks." Oh dear! When we got to my room, I invited him in, and we talked for a long time. I was getting sleepy, but he seemed to need to talk, so I tried to stay awake. Finally, he got up to go. At the door, he hugged me and kissed me on the forehead. It was just a friendly kiss.

After he left, I thought, *I'll probably never see him again. Too bad, too, as he is so full of muscle, and good-looking.*

I remembered when he helped move Mike and me up from Eugene to Salem a few years earlier and we were eating at the Dairy Queen, I looked at him and thought, *He is so kind and unselfish and good-looking.* He was tall, six feet two, dark, and handsome. I had asked the Lord, "Could you find me a clone of him? He is really nice."

Here it was a few years later, in the middle of the week, and my phone was ringing with Dale on the other end. It wasn't a clone but the real thing.

"I have been out kicking gravel."

I had no idea what that meant. I didn't know if that was good or bad.

"Would you like to go out to dinner with me Saturday night? I'll pick you up at seven if you would."

We were such good friends, and I thought a date might spoil it all. In spite of that, I heard myself saying, "I'll be ready."

After I hung up, I thought, *Is this going to be a date?*

He was a wonderful man, but did I really want to date anyone? I was happy eating with my girls and had no need to go out on dates anymore. I figured we would probably go dancing afterwards, so that would be fun. I really enjoyed moving to music. I told myself that I had committed myself now, so better make the best of it.

I was due to go in to see the pastor again so thought I would mention my upcoming date.

"Joanne, don't be afraid to date Dale. He is a good man. He deserves a good woman."

I guess he was considering me a good woman. I remembered that my John, before he died, had told me what a good man Dale was. He respected him. He was a man's man.

With those thoughts in my mind, I opened the door and smiled at my handsome truck driver date. He was right on time. (I soon learned that was a nice trait of his. He could give estimated times of arrival almost down to the minute, even if he still had hundreds of miles yet to travel.) I heard some of the girls behind me whispering as they checked out my date. I knew I would hear of their approval or disapproval the next day.

He opened my car door and was a perfect gentleman. He had made reservations at one of the nicest restaurants in town. Our table was right over the river. We had such a lovely view. *However,* I found I was nervous on this "date." We both had trouble being ourselves. Finally, after strained conversation, I suggested, "This is awful. May we please just be friends as we always have been? I think it would be more fun than a date."

"Sure, I just wanted to be with you!"

The rest of the dinner went great, and we laughed and talked freely. After dinner, he did drive to another restaurant where they had a dance floor and band. We were soon dancing every dance, and the time just slipped away. I didn't realize he had to get up at three AM to go to work the next day. He didn't say a word about it. We finally left and headed toward my sorority. He parked in the alley and reached over to give me a kiss. *Wow*, sparks really flew!

"So much for just friendship," I muttered.

I saw girls hanging out all the windows. Just as our lips met again, a police car drove up behind us and turned on his flashing red lights. I prayed he wouldn't turn on his siren. There was a knock on Dale's window, and there stood the policeman that I had seen many times when he came to rescue my girls. He saw me, saw Dale, and said, "Better not park in the alley."

And then he left. I scooted out and ran into the house. I was greeted by a houseful of giggling girls.

"We would have sprung you from jail," they laughed.

They all waved as Dale drove out of the alley, I thought maybe never to be seen again.

What a start to a romantic friendship, I thought.

"He probably won't ever date me again," I lamented to my girls as I went into my little room.

He did call later that week for a date. That date, however, went a little better. He asked me out to breakfast and a walk by the river before taking me to church. Oh! That was so nice.

"Why did you wait eight years to date me?" I asked after another of his wonderful kisses.

"You don't date your minister's wife." He winked.

Dale and I enjoyed going to all the football games As there were several cheerleaders in the house, it meant that when we went to the football games, they would come running over and hug us, yelling, "Hi, Mom! Hi, Dad!" They just included Dale too.

Dale really liked this! They all hugged and kissed him on the forehead or cheek also.

"I sure hope some of my fellow truckers are watching. They won't believe this." He grinned.

He began hanging around the sorority and helping the girls with their projects. He enjoyed it, and they loved having him help out.

While we were walking in the mall, some of my young ladies would come up and greet us with hugs and kisses and call him Dad. He loved it. *Maybe that's why he wants to stick around,* I thought.

One day, while walking in the mall, we passed a jewelry store, and he guided me in.

"Let's look for rings. Do you like that one?"

It was a beautiful ring with a big diamond in the middle

and several diamonds all around. I sure hoped he had looked at the price and it was what he had in mind to spend, because I was in awe. He could tell by my face. As he was a big man, I knew he would need a big ring. We found the perfect one.

As he had not asked me to marry him yet, I figured he just wanted to see what I liked. I was shocked when he pulled out his wallet and we left them to be sized.

On the way home, I mentioned that probably not too many couples buy wedding rings before the fellow asks the girl to marry him.

"I've already called your folks and asked them for their blessing on our marriage, and they gave it to me." I couldn't believe my folks hadn't told me.

"Do you think you might have left out a step in this somewhere? Like asking someone to marry you?"

"I just thought it was a mutual understanding."

We were engaged for six wonderful months. I finished the school year with my sorority and with Dale coming over all the time and helping the girls with many of their fun projects.

Now, when any of the ladies in the house got engaged, they had a special ceremony. They would put the ring on a cone and pass it all around the room and then try to guess who it belonged to. So I decided to do that also. Everyone held it and tried to guess who had gotten engaged. My ring went all around the room with ohs and ahhs until it almost got back to me. Then they all shouted at once.

"Mom, it's you!"

"How did you know it was mine?"

"None of the college students we date could afford a ring like that," they answered in chorus.

Also, the fellow was supposed to furnish evening treats for the whole house. So Dale had lots of pizza delivered for everyone. They loved it. He got lots of hugs and kisses the next time he came over. He was really being accepted, and he loved it. So did I. He was such a wonderful man!

The sorority asked me if I would consider coming back next year as a married couple.

"No way! I didn't just fall off the turnip truck."

Just before the end of school, Dale told me, "Honey, please go to a travel agency and get info on Hawaii. That's where I want to take you on our honeymoon."

The very next day, I did that and hurried back to my apartment to read the brochures. As I sat reading the literature, my eyes fell on my journal. I opened it, and it fell to the page in January where I had asked God for a sign that He was real. I remembered that He had had me write down what I wanted. I had said, "Go to Hawaii and not with my parents." Well, here I was reading about Hawaii for my honeymoon. I got goose bumps. *Yes! My God is real, and He cares about me. He is not only all-powerful, but He is sweet too.*

I took this to mean I had found the man who would stay and eat cinnamon rolls for life. *And he did!* But that's a whole new story.